BAKE
good
THINGS

FROM THE EDITORS OF
WILLIAMS-SONOMA

PHOTOGRAPHS BY EVA KOLENKO

weldon**owen**

CONTENTS

BAKE *good* STUFF TODAY

If you're ready to take your baking skills up a notch, and move beyond boxed brownies, grocery-store cakes with brightly colored icing, and frozen pizza, we're here to help. With this book as your guide, you'll become more confident in the kitchen and up your baking game, while having fun along the way.

Within these pages are straightforward lessons for learning to master cookies & bars; muffins & quickbreads; biscuits, scones & cobblers; pies; cakes & cupcakes; and breads & pizzas—all of which can be done with just a few basic kitchen items—no special equipment is needed. Each easy-to-understand lesson presents the key tools you'll

If there's one takeaway from reading this book, it's simply that you'll learn to bake good things.

need, the secrets of success for that method, and answers to common baking questions. We've also included step-by-step instructions with full-color photos, so there's no mystery involved in the process. Don't worry about learning to frost a multi-tiered cake—the techniques in this book are easy, yet still impressive.

Each baking lesson is followed by ten recipes for delicious sweet and savory baked goods that are fit for everyday noshing, hosting a brunch, or even a special celebration. And you'll enjoy baking these dishes as much as eating them. Use this book as your personal kitchen handbook, a go-to collection of reliable recipes, or both—it's up to you. But if there's one takeaway from reading this book, it's simply that you'll learn to bake good things.

COOKIES & BARS

ALL ABOUT
COOKIES
& BARS

From chocolate chip to shortbread, brownies to lemon bars, cookies and bars have more in common than just being handheld sweets. Many of these recipes use a common mixing method: creaming. Creaming is done in the beginning stages of many cookie batters to create a smooth, uniform mixture. This step also helps ensure a soft, lump-free batter, and a pleasing texture after baking.

Creaming involves beating together butter and sugar until a light, smooth mixture is formed. This important step creates cookies with an even, consistent texture.

Creaming ingredients is best done with an electric mixer, which will help the fat (usually butter) and sugar distribute evenly throughout the batter. To ensure you are creaming sufficiently, use medium speed on your mixer and set the kitchen timer for 2 minutes.

Creaming isn't the only essential step in creating these perfect treats. Other not-to-be-missed steps that can be applied to cookies or bars include: beating eggs until well combined; spacing cookie dough generously and evenly on room temperature baking sheets; rotating baking sheets or pans in the oven halfway through baking time; and letting cookies and bars cool slightly on the pan before serving or before transferring to a wire rack to cool completely.

WHAT DOES "ALL-PURPOSE FLOUR" MEAN?

When it comes to cookies, unbleached all-purpose flour is the norm. A mixture of soft and hard wheats, all-purpose flour produces the most consistent results in a variety of different types of recipes. We like unbleached all-purpose flour, as it hasn't been chemically treated or processed.

SECRETS TO SUCCESS

SPACE OUT To make sure cookies don't run together on the baking sheet in the hot oven, space the dough mounds 1–2 inches (2.5–5 cm) apart on all sides.

ARE THEY DONE YET? Depending on your oven, cookies may need a little less or a little more baking time than called for in the recipe. Check the cookies about 5 minutes before the recommended baking time is up.

HANDLE WITH CARE When baking bars, such as brownies and lemon bars, line the pans with parchment paper: Cut two opposite sides to fit the pan, and cut the remaining two sides so that the parchment extends 2 inches (5 cm) above the pan. Use the parchment "handles" to help ease the bars out of the pan before cutting.

TWO-STEP COOLING Always cool cookies partially on the baking sheet to prevent crumbling, then transfer them to a cooling rack.

COOL YOUR SHEETS If you're using the same baking sheet for multiple batches of cookies, let the sheet cool fully before adding fresh dough.

THE MODERN COOKIE JAR Cookies and bars should be stored in an airtight container, in a cool, dark place. If you're transporting them, load up the container so that there is less room for them to move and break.

STICKING POINTS

There are two options for keeping your cookies from sticking to the baking sheet: parchment paper or a silicone baking mat. Parchment paper is economical, can be cut to fit any baking sheet or pan, and makes for easy cleanup. But if you're an avid baker, a silicone mat—a reusable, nonstick baking mat—might be a good investment.

WHAT YOU NEED

ASSORTED MIXING BOWLS

METAL SIEVE OR SIFTER (OPTIONAL)

ELECTRIC MIXER OR WHISK

WOODEN SPOON

BAKING SHEET

METAL SPATULA

WIRE COOLING RACK

HOW TO MAKE
COOKIES

1
MIX DRY INGREDIENTS
Use a fine-mesh sieve, if called
for, or stir together the flour,
salt, baking powder or soda, and
other ingredients in a bowl.

2
CREAM BUTTER & SUGAR
Using an electric mixer on
medium speed, beat until the
ingredients are smooth and
creamy, about 2 minutes.

3
ADD EGGS & FLAVORINGS
Add the eggs and vanilla
extract or other flavorings,
and beat until combined.

4
FINISH THE DOUGH
Switch to a wooden spoon and stir in the dry ingredients and any additions, such as chocolate chips.

5
PORTION
Use two spoons (or a small ice cream scoop) to portion the dough onto a parchment-lined pan, leaving 1–2 inches (2.5–5 cm) of space between each dough mound.

6
COOL & ENJOY
After a brief cooling period on the baking sheet, use a metal spatula to transfer cookies to a wire rack to cool slightly or completely.

CHOCOLATE CHIP COOKIES

MAKES 30 COOKIES

Just like Mom made them—and infinitely better than store-bought dough—these classic cookies are exactly what you expect them to be: soft, with a tinge of caramel flavor, and studded with chocolate goodness. Be sure not to crowd the dough on the baking sheets, as the cookies will expand quite a bit as they bake.

1 Preheat the oven to 350°F (180°C). Line 2 baking sheets with parchment paper.

2 In a bowl, sift together the flour, baking soda, and salt. In a large bowl, using an electric mixer on medium speed, beat the butter, brown sugar, and granulated sugar until smooth, about 2 minutes. Add the egg and vanilla and mix on low speed until blended. Slowly add the flour mixture and mix just until incorporated. Switch to a wooden spoon and stir in the chocolate chips.

3 Using a small ice cream scoop or heaping tablespoon, drop the dough onto the prepared baking sheets, spacing the dough mounds 2 inches (5 cm) apart.

4 Bake the cookies, 1 sheet at a time, until the bottoms and edges are lightly browned and the tops feel firm when lightly touched, 10–13 minutes. Let the cookies cool on the baking sheets for 5 minutes, then transfer the cookies to wire racks to cool completely.

Unbleached all-purpose flour, 1¼ cups (6½ oz/200 g)

Baking soda, 1 teaspoon

Salt, ½ teaspoon

Unsalted butter, ½ cup (1 stick/4 oz/125 g), at room temperature

Light brown sugar, ½ cup (3½ oz/105 g), firmly packed

Granulated sugar, 6 tablespoons (3 oz/90 g)

Large egg, 1

Vanilla extract, 1 teaspoon

Semisweet chocolate chips, 2½ cups (15 oz/470 g)

{ **FORMING THE PERFECT COOKIES**
Ever wonder how bakeries form their cookies into perfect rounds? You, too, can create shapely cookies with the aid of an ice cream scoop. Fill a small ice cream scoop with dough, press it with the palm of your hand into a uniform mound, release the dough onto a parchment-lined baking sheet, and voilà! Consistently gorgeous cookies every time.

CHOCOLATE EARTHQUAKE COOKIES

MAKES 30 COOKIES

With a crisp, black-and-white crackled exterior and a chewy, fudgy interior, these cookies satisfy any chocolate craving. Their appearance resembles pavement cracks after an earthquake, hence the name. For best results, be sure to refrigerate the batter until it's firm enough to form into balls.

1 Place the chocolate and butter in a heatproof bowl. Microwave on low for 1 minute. Stir and continue to microwave on low in 30-second bursts, stirring in between intervals, until the butter and chocolate are melted and smooth. Set aside to cool slightly.

2 In a bowl, stir together the flour, cocoa powder, baking powder, and salt. In a large bowl, using an electric mixer on medium speed, beat the eggs, granulated sugar, and vanilla until the mixture is light in color and thickened, about 3 minutes. Add the melted chocolate mixture and mix on low speed until blended. Add the flour mixture and beat on low until incorporated. Switch to a wooden spoon and stir in the chocolate chips. Cover the bowl with plastic wrap and refrigerate until the dough is firm, about 2 hours.

3 Preheat the oven to 325°F (165°C). Line 2 baking sheets with parchment paper. Sift the confectioners' sugar into a small bowl.

4 To form each cookie, roll a rounded tablespoon of dough between your palms into a 1½-inch (4-cm) ball, and then roll the ball in the confectioners' sugar. Place the balls 3 inches (7.5 cm) apart on the prepared baking sheets, pressing them firmly onto the sheet to stay in place.

5 Bake the cookies, 1 sheet at a time, until the tops are puffed and crinkled and feel firm when lightly touched, 13–17 minutes. Let the cookies cool on the baking sheets for 5 minutes, then transfer the cookies to wire racks to cool completely.

Unsweetened chocolate, 4 oz (125 g), chopped

Unsalted butter, ¼ cup (½ stick/2 oz/60 g)

Unbleached all-purpose flour, 1½ cups (7½ oz/235 g)

Unsweetened Dutch-process cocoa powder, ½ cup (1½ oz/45 g)

Baking powder, 2 teaspoons

Salt, ¼ teaspoon

Large eggs, 4

Granulated sugar, 2 cups (1 lb/500 g)

Vanilla extract, 1 teaspoon

Miniature semisweet chocolate chips, 1½ cups (9 oz/280 g)

Confectioners' sugar, ½ cup (2 oz/60 g)

TROPICAL LIME SHORTBREAD

Shortbread is one of the easiest cookies to make and only calls for a few ingredients. A good shortbread cookie should be buttery, tender, and slightly crumbly, but still have some crunch. This recipe gives classic shortbread a Caribbean twist with sweet toasted coconut and freshly grated lime zest.

1 Preheat the oven to 350°F (190°C). Spread the coconut on a baking sheet and toast in the oven, stirring occasionally, until it is lightly golden, about 5 minutes. Set aside. Reduce the oven temperature to 325°F (165°C).

2 In a bowl, using an electric mixer on medium speed, beat the butter and the ⅓ cup (3 oz/90 g) sugar until smooth, about 2 minutes. Add the lime zest and salt and beat on low speed until combined. Add the toasted coconut and flour and beat on low just until the dough comes together. Dump the dough onto a large piece of parchment paper, top with another large piece of parchment paper, and roll out the dough into a rectangle about ¼ inch (6 mm) thick. Put the parchment-covered dough on a baking sheet and refrigerate for about 30 minutes.

3 Slide the dough onto a work surface. Remove the top piece of parchment and use it to line a baking sheet.

4 Cut the dough into rectangles measuring about 1-by-3 inches (2.5-by-7.5 cm). Transfer them to the prepared baking sheet, spacing the dough pieces slightly apart. Pierce the surface of the dough all over with a fork and sprinkle lightly with sugar. Bake the cookies until lightly golden at the edges, about 22 minutes. Let the cookies cool on the pan for 5 minutes, then transfer to wire racks to cool completely.

Sweetened shredded coconut, ⅓ cup (1½ oz/45 g), packed

Unsalted butter, ¾ cup (1½ sticks/6 oz/185 g), at room temperature

Sugar, ⅓ cup (3 oz/90 g), plus extra as needed

Lime zest, finely grated from 1 large lime

Salt, ½ teaspoon

Unbleached all-purpose flour, 1⅓ cups (7 oz/220 g)

{ **PREP WORK: ZESTING CITRUS FRUITS**
Wash the citrus well. Use a Microplane grater or the small grating holes on a box grater to remove only the colored portion of the peel, avoiding the bitter white pith underneath.

SCOTTISH-STYLE SHORTBREAD

These classic Scottish-style cookies will melt in your mouth. You probably already have the ingredients on hand in your pantry to make them, and they are easy to mix and easy to shape—simply press them into a pan with your fingers. If you only have salted butter on hand, go ahead and use it—just cut back a bit on the salt.

1 Preheat the oven to 300°F (150°C). Have ready an ungreased 9-inch (23-cm) square baking pan.

2 In a large bowl, using an electric mixer on medium speed, beat the butter until fluffy and pale yellow. Add the confectioners' sugar and the ¼ cup (2 oz/60 g) granulated sugar and continue beating until the mixture is no longer gritty when rubbed between your finger and thumb, 2–3 minutes. Beat in the vanilla.

3 In a bowl, sift together the flour and salt. Gradually add the flour mixture to the butter mixture and mix on low speed just until blended.

4 Using floured fingertips, press the dough evenly into the pan. Sprinkle evenly with the remaining 1 tablespoon granulated sugar. Bake the shortbread until the edges are golden, about 1 hour.

5 Remove the pan from the oven and immediately use a thin, sharp knife to cut the shortbread into rectangles measuring about 1-by-3 inches (2.5-by-7.5 cm). Press the tines of a fork into the surface of each shortbread a few times to give it a decorative pattern. Let the rectangles cool in the pan on a wire rack for 30 minutes. Then, transfer the rectangles to a wire rack to cool completely.

Unsalted butter, 1 cup (2 sticks/8 oz/250 g), at room temperature

Confectioners' sugar, ¼ cup (1 oz/30 g)

Granulated sugar, ¼ cup (2 oz/60 g), plus 1 tablespoon for sprinkling

Vanilla extract, 2 teaspoons

Unbleached all-purpose flour, 1½ cups (7½ oz/235 g)

Salt, ¼ teaspoon

DOUBLE-GINGER GINGERSNAPS

MAKES 4 DOZEN COOKIES

These delightfully spiced cookies get their bold flavor and chewy texture from the addition of two forms of ginger: ground ginger and crystallized ginger. Here's a good baking tip: Measure the oil in a glass measuring cup, then use the same cup to measure the molasses, which will help it flow freely from the cup.

1 Preheat the oven to 325°F (165°C). Line 2 baking sheets with parchment paper.

2 In a bowl, sift together the flour, ground ginger, baking soda, cinnamon, cloves, and salt.

3 In a large bowl, using a wooden spoon, stir together the oil, brown sugar, and molasses until well blended. Add the whole beaten egg and beat until blended. Stir in the flour mixture and the crystallized ginger.

4 Lightly beat the egg white in a small bowl. Spread the sugar crystals in a shallow bowl. With dampened hands, shape the dough into 1-inch (2.5-cm) balls. Brush each ball lightly with the egg white and roll in the sugar to lightly coat. Place the cookies about 1 inch (2.5 cm) apart on the prepared sheets. Bake until the tops of the cookies are set and crackled, 15–18 minutes.

5 Let the cookies cool on the baking sheets on wire racks for 5 minutes, then transfer the cookies to wire racks to cool completely. The cookies will firm as they cool.

{ INGREDIENT DEMYSTIFIED: CRYSTALLIZED GINGER Crystallized ginger is sliced or roughly chopped fresh ginger that has been candied in sugar syrup and then coated with granulated sugar. Look for it in specialty food stores or upscale markets.

Unbleached all-purpose flour, 2½ cups (12½ oz/390 g)

Ground ginger, 1½ teaspoons

Baking soda, 1 teaspoon

Ground cinnamon, ½ teaspoon

Ground cloves, ¼ teaspoon

Salt, ¼ teaspoon

Canola oil, ⅔ cup (5 fl oz/160 ml)

Light brown sugar, 1 cup (7 oz/220 g), firmly packed

Dark molasses, ⅓ cup (3½ oz/115 g)

Large egg, 1, lightly beaten

Crystallized ginger, ¾ cup (4½ oz/140 g) chopped

Large egg white, 1

Coarse sugar crystals, ½ cup (4 oz/125 g)

CHOCOLATE–PEANUT BUTTER COOKIE SANDWICHES

MAKES 3 DOZEN COOKIE SANDWICHES

Perhaps one of the most timeless and beloved sweet combinations ever, chocolate and peanut butter never fail to deliver on deliciousness. Here, we've sandwiched the creamy, nutty filling between two soft chocolate cookies. The best part is, they can be eaten immediately after assembling, if you don't start in on them sooner.

1 To make the cookies, in a large bowl, using an electric mixer on medium speed, beat the butter until fluffy and pale. Add the granulated sugar and continue beating until the mixture is no longer gritty when rubbed between your finger and thumb, 2–3 minutes. Add the eggs and vanilla and stir or beat on low speed until blended.

2 In a bowl, sift together the flour, cocoa, baking powder, baking soda, and salt. Add the flour mixture to the butter mixture and beat on low speed just until blended. Cover the bowl with plastic wrap and refrigerate until the dough is firm, about 2 hours.

3 Preheat the oven to 350°F (180°C). Line 2 baking sheets with parchment paper.

4 With dampened hands, shape the dough into ¾-inch (2-cm) balls, and place them 2 inches (5 cm) apart on the prepared baking sheets. Using a spatula, press down on each dough ball to flatten it slightly. Bake the cookies until the surface is firm when lightly touched, 10–12 minutes. Let the cookies cool on the baking sheets for 5 minutes, then transfer the cookies to wire racks to cool completely; they will be soft.

5 To make the filling, in a large bowl, combine the butter, confectioners' sugar, peanut butter, and vanilla. Using the mixer and clean beaters, beat on low speed until blended and smooth. Cover and refrigerate until the cookies are cool.

6 Spread the flat side of half the cookies with 1½ teaspoons of the filling. Top each with a second cookie, flat side down. Press lightly to make a cookie sandwich.

FOR THE COOKIES

Unsalted butter, ¾ cup (1½ sticks/6 oz/185 g), at room temperature

Granulated sugar, ¾ cup (6 oz/185 g)

Large eggs, 2

Vanilla extract, 1 teaspoon

Unbleached all-purpose flour, ½ cup (2½ oz/75 g)

Unsweetened Dutch-process cocoa powder, ½ cup (1½ oz/45 g)

Baking powder, ¼ teaspoon

Baking soda, ¼ teaspoon

Salt, ⅛ teaspoon

FOR THE FILLING

Unsalted butter, 4 tablespoons (2 oz/60 g), at room temperature

Confectioners' sugar, ½ cup (2 oz/60 g)

Creamy peanut butter, ½ cup (5 oz/155 g)

Vanilla extract, ½ teaspoon

COCONUT-LEMON BARS

MAKES 48 RECTANGLES

This recipe takes regular lemon bars and kicks them up a notch by mixing shredded coconut into the creamy lemon curd filling. The flaky crust comes together quick and easy with the aid of a hand mixer. If you really like coconut, sprinkle extra toasted coconut on top of the cooled bars for extra sweetness and texture.

1 Preheat the oven to 325°F (165°C). Line a 13-by-9-by-2-inch (33-by-23-by-5-cm) baking pan with parchment paper, letting some excess parchment extend up 2 opposite sides of the pan.

2 To make the crust, in a large bowl, stir together the flour, confectioners' sugar, lemon zest, and salt. Using a pastry blender or 2 butter knives, cut in the butter just until the mixture forms large, coarse crumbs the size of small peas. Firmly and evenly press the dough mixture over the bottom and 1 inch (2.5 cm) up the sides of the prepared pan. Bake just until the edges are lightly browned, about 20 minutes. Set aside. Reduce the oven temperature to 300°F (150°C).

3 To make the filling, in a large bowl, whisk the eggs just until blended. Add the granulated sugar and lemon juice and zest and whisk until smooth, about 1 minute. Add the coconut and mix well. Sift the flour into the bowl and whisk until incorporated.

4 Slowly pour the filling over the crust. Bake until the filling looks set and does not wobble when the pan is shaken, 40–45 minutes. Transfer the pan to a wire rack and let cool until room temperature, about 1 hour. Cover the pan with plastic wrap and refrigerate until firm, at least 4 hours.

5 Holding the ends of the parchment, lift the bar onto a cutting surface. Using a large, sharp knife, cut the bar into 48 rectangles.

FOR THE CRUST

Unbleached all-purpose flour, 1½ cups (7½ oz/235 g)

Confectioners' sugar, ½ cup (2 oz/60 g)

Lemon zest, 1½ teaspoons, finely grated

Salt, ⅛ teaspoon

Cold unsalted butter, ¾ cup (1½ sticks/6 oz/185 g), cut into ½-inch (12-mm) pieces

FOR THE FILLING

Large eggs, 6

Granulated sugar, 2½ cups (1 lb 4 oz/625 g)

Fresh lemon juice, ¾ cup (6 fl oz/180 ml)

Lemon zest, 1 tablespoon finely grated

Sweetened shredded coconut, 2 cups (8 oz/250 g)

Unbleached all-purpose flour, ½ cup (2½ oz/75 g)

CARAMEL-GLAZED BLONDIES

Brownies' lighter, cocoa-free cousins, blondies get a sweet upgrade when drizzled with an easy caramel-flavored glaze. If you are adventurous, try adding a sprinkle or two of salt to the finished caramel before spreading it onto the blondies for a tempting contrast of sweet and salty flavors.

1 Preheat the oven to 325°F (165°C). Line an 8-inch (20-cm) square baking pan with parchment paper, letting some excess parchment extend up 2 opposite sides of the pan.

2 To make the blondies, in a saucepan over medium heat, combine the butter and brown sugar. Warm, stirring often, until the butter is melted and the mixture is smooth. Scrape the mixture into a large bowl and let cool slightly.

3 In a small bowl, sift together the flour, baking powder, and salt. Add the eggs and vanilla to the sugar mixture and use a large spoon to mix until smooth. Add the flour mixture and stir just until incorporated to make a batter. Pour the batter into the prepared pan, using a silicone spatula to spread the top evenly. Bake until a toothpick inserted in the center comes out with moist crumbs attached, 20–25 minutes. Transfer the pan to a wire rack and let cool until room temperature, about 1 hour.

4 To make the glaze, in a saucepan over medium heat, combine the brown sugar, heavy cream, and butter. Warm, stirring constantly, until the butter is melted and the mixture is smooth. Raise the heat to medium-high and boil for 2 minutes. Remove from the heat and stir in the vanilla. Let cool. Sift the confectioners' sugar into a bowl, then whisk in the cooled brown sugar mixture to make a smooth glaze. Spread the glaze evenly over the cooled blondie, still in the pan. Let stand until set, about 30 minutes.

5 Holding the ends of the parchment, lift the blondie onto a cutting surface. Run a large knife under hot running water and wipe clean, then use it to cut the blondie into 24 rectangles.

FOR THE BLONDIES

Unsalted butter, ½ cup (1 stick/4 oz/125 g)

Light brown sugar, 1½ cups (10½ oz/330 g), firmly packed

Unbleached all-purpose flour, 1½ cups (7½ oz/235 g)

Baking powder, 1 teaspoon

Salt, ¼ teaspoon

Large eggs, 2

Vanilla extract, 1 teaspoon

FOR THE CARAMEL GLAZE

Dark brown sugar, ¾ cup (6 oz/185 g) firmly packed

Heavy cream, ½ cup (4 fl oz/125 ml)

Unsalted butter, ¼ cup (½ stick/2 oz/60 g)

Vanilla extract, 1 teaspoon

Confectioners' sugar, ½ cup (2 oz/60 g)

DARK CHOCOLATE BROWNIES

MAKES 24 RECTANGLES

These intensely chocolaty brownies boast the prerequisite chewy goodness and crisp corners, but with a luxurious twist: Unsweetened chocolate adds a deeper flavor than its sweeter, milkier counterparts. If you are licking the bowl, don't be put off by the taste of the raw chocolate, which is completely transformed once baked.

1 Preheat the oven to 350°F (180°C). Line an 8-inch (20-cm) square baking pan with parchment paper, letting some excess parchment extend up 2 opposite sides of the pan.

2 Place the chocolate and butter in a heatproof bowl. Microwave on low for 1 minute. Stir and continue to microwave on low in 30-second bursts, stirring in between intervals, until the butter and chocolate are melted and smooth. Set aside to cool slightly.

3 In a large bowl, whisk together the eggs, sugar, salt, and vanilla until blended. Whisk in the chocolate mixture. Sprinkle all the flour over the mixture and whisk slowly just until blended. Pour the batter into the prepared pan, using a silicone spatula to spread the top evenly.

4 Bake until a toothpick inserted into the center comes out almost clean or with a few moist crumbs attached to it, 35–40 minutes. Be careful not to overbake. Transfer the pan to a wire rack to let cool completely.

5 Holding the ends of the parchment, lift the brownie onto a cutting surface. Using a large, sharp knife, cut into 24 rectangles. If desired, dust with cocoa powder or confectioners' sugar.

Unsweetened chocolate, 6 oz (185 g), chopped

Unsalted butter, ¾ cup (1½ sticks/6 oz/185 g), cut into ¾-inch (2-cm) pieces

Large eggs, 3

Sugar, 1¼ cups (10 oz/315 g)

Salt, ¼ teaspoon

Vanilla extract, 2 teaspoons

Unbleached all-purpose flour, 1 cup (5 oz/155 g) plus 2 tablespoons

Unsweetened cocoa powder or confectioners' sugar, for dusting (optional)

{ **PREP WORK: CHOPPING CHOCOLATE**
Chocolate melts best when it's chopped into small, evenly sized pieces. Using a serrated knife (aka a bread knife), cut the chocolate into small, even pieces. If you don't have a serrated knife, a large chef's knife will work well, too, but it may take longer to chop.

OATMEAL STREUSEL JAM BARS

The great thing about these crave-worthy bars is that you only have to make one dough: Part of it is pressed into the pan bottom for the crust, and the rest serves as the crunchy streusel topping. Sandwiched in between is a thick layer of sweet-tart jam. Substitute any favorite flavor for the raspberry jam, if you like.

1 Preheat the oven to 350°F (180°C). Generously butter a 9-by-13-inch (23-by-33-cm) baking pan.

2 In a food processor, combine the flour, sugar, butter, vanilla, cinnamon, salt, baking soda, and orange zest. Pulse until the mixture forms coarse crumbs. Add the oats and pulse a few times to mix.

3 Firmly press about two-thirds of the oat mixture into the bottom of the prepared pan so it holds together. Using a spatula, spread the jam evenly over the top. Sprinkle the remaining oat mixture over the jam to form a crumbly topping. Bake until the top is golden and the jam is bubbling, 35–40 minutes.

4 Transfer the pan to a wire rack to cool completely. Using a large knife, cut it into 20 squares.

{ **FANCY FOOD TERM: STREUSEL**
"Streusel" is a German word that refers to a crumbly mixture of flour, butter, and sugar. It's often used as a crunchy, sweet topping for crumbles, cakes, and, popularly, coffee cake. Nuts, rolled oats, and ground spices are sometimes added to streusel for texture and flavor.

Unbleached all-purpose flour, 1⅔ cups (9 oz/275 g)

Light brown sugar, 1 cup (7 oz/220 g) firmly packed

Cold unsalted butter, ¾ cup (1½ sticks/6 oz/185 g), cut into chunks

Vanilla extract, 2 teaspoons

Ground cinnamon, 1 teaspoon

Salt, ½ teaspoon

Baking soda, ¼ teaspoon

Orange zest, finely grated from 1 small orange

Rolled oats, 1⅔ cups (5 oz/155 g)

Raspberry jam, 1½ cups (15 oz/470 g)

MUFFINS & QUICKBREADS

ALL ABOUT
MUFFINS &
QUICKBREADS

From sweet to savory, muffins and quickbreads are crowd-pleasing favorites. They make fast and easy breakfasts paired with a cup of coffee, or delicious accompaniments to a savory meal. If you are a novice baker, you can relax knowing that these are some of the simplest, most foolproof baked goods to assemble, and they require little more than stirring together a handful of everyday ingredients.

Muffin-making requires three basic mixing techniques: creaming the butter, combining the dry ingredients, and then blending them together with some form of liquid.

These types of baked goods are usually made in a three-step process: First, the sugar and butter are creamed together (see page 12); next, the dry ingredients are stirred together; finally, the two elements are combined with a wet ingredient and gently mixed. After the first three components are combined to make a batter, any additions, such as chocolate chips, crumbled cheeses, dried fruit, or similar items, are mixed in, creating endless variations.

Muffins and quickbreads typically use baking powder or baking soda as the leavening agent to help create air bubbles to ensure that they rise. After the addition of the leavening agent, batters should be baked as soon as possible for best flavor and texture.

WHAT'S A STANDARD MUFFIN PAN?

A standard muffin pan refers to a pan with 12 muffin cups, each about 1 inch (2.5 cm) deep and 3 inches (7.5 cm) in diameter. All the recipes in this book call for standard muffin cups, but you can also find mini and jumbo muffin pans in cookware stores. They require different baking times than standard muffin pans.

SECRETS TO SUCCESS

PREP WORK
Before making the batter, prepare your pan according to the recipe instructions.

DON'T OVERMIX
Overmixing can result in dense muffins or quickbreads with tough crumbs. Be sure to use a light hand when mixing and mix until the ingredients are just incorporated.

DONENESS TEST
To check for doneness, insert a clean toothpick or skewer in the center of a muffin. If it comes out clean, they're ready! If not, pop them back in the oven for a few more minutes and check again.

DEALING WITH STUBBORN MUFFINS
Paper liners help muffins slide out with ease. But if some batter spills over the sides and your muffins are stuck in the pan, slide a butter knife around the perimeter between the paper and the muffin cup to slide them free.

PAN SIZE MATTERS To ensure even baking, it's important to use the right pan size called for in recipes: A too-small pan will cause overflow and dripping and a too-large pan will result in unsightly, flat-topped muffins and breads.

BAKING SODA VS. BAKING POWDER

Baking powder and baking soda have distinct roles in baked goods and are not interchangeable. Baking soda works when it comes in contact with an acidic substance, such as buttermilk, to produce carbon dioxide bubbles that produce tender baked goods. Baking powder is a combination of baking soda, an acid, and a moisture-absorber that works to release gases in the wet batter.

ASSORTED MIXING BOWLS

ELECTRIC MIXER OR WHISK

SILICONE SPATULA OR WOODEN SPOON

MUFFIN PAN OR LOAF PAN

ICE CREAM SCOOP

SKEWER OR TOOTHPICK

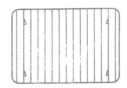

WIRE COOLING RACK

HOW TO MAKE
MUFFINS

1

PREPARE THE PAN
For muffins, use paper liners.
For loaf pans, spray with cooking
spray, spread with butter,
or line with parchment.

2

CREATE BATTER
ELEMENTS
Mix wet ingredients and
dry ingredients separately
sifting the dry ingredients,
through a fine-mesh
sieve if necessary.

3

FINISH THE BATTER
Combine the batter elements,
alternating with the liquid
element or egg mixture.
Take care not to overmix.

4

FILL & BAKE

Fill the pan with the batter.
An ice cream scoop fills
muffin cups mess-free.

5

TEST FOR DONENESS

Insert a skewer or toothpick into
the center. If it comes out clean,
the baked good is done. If it comes
out wet, bake for a few more
minutes and check again.

6

UNMOLD & COOL

Let cool in the pan for a
few minutes, then unmold
onto a wire rack to cool
the rest of the way.

BROWN SUGAR STREUSEL MUFFINS

MAKES 12 MUFFINS

Tender on the inside, and capped by a sweet, buttery topping, these treats pack all the best elements of coffee cake into personal-sized muffins. They're great for breakfast, lunch, or even snacks, and are a popular addition to a Sunday brunch with friends. Mimosas, anyone?

1 Preheat the oven to 400°F (200°C). Line 12 standard muffin cups with paper liners.

2 To make the streusel, in a bowl, stir together the flour and brown sugar. Scatter the butter over the top and work it in with your hands until the mixture forms small chunks. Freeze the streusel while you make the batter.

3 To make the batter, in a bowl, sift together the flour, baking powder, baking soda, and salt. In a large bowl, combine the butter and granulated sugar. Using an electric mixer on medium speed, beat until smooth, about 2 minutes. Add the eggs, one at a time, and beat until well combined, scraping down the sides of the bowl with a rubber spatula. Beat in the vanilla. Add the sour cream and beat on low speed just until combined. Add the flour mixture and, using the rubber spatula, stir it into the batter just until evenly moistened. The batter will be thick.

4 Spoon the batter into each muffin cup, filling it about two-thirds full. Sprinkle the streusel evenly over the tops. Bake until golden-brown and a toothpick inserted into the center of a muffin comes out clean, about 15 minutes.

5 Let the muffins cool in the pan on a wire rack for about 5 minutes, then turn onto the rack to cool a bit more. Serve warm.

FOR THE STREUSEL

Unbleached all-purpose flour, ¼ cup (1½ oz/45 g)

Light brown sugar, ¼ cup (2 oz/60 g) firmly packed

Cold unsalted butter, 3 tablespoons, cut into chunks

FOR THE BATTER

Unbleached all-purpose flour, 2 cups (10 oz/315 g)

Baking powder, 2 teaspoons

Baking soda, ½ teaspoon

Salt, ¼ teaspoon

Unsalted butter, ½ cup (1 stick/4 oz/125 g), at room temperature

Granulated sugar, ½ cup (4 oz/125 g)

Large eggs, 2

Vanilla extract, 2 teaspoons

Sour cream, 1 cup (8 oz/250 g)

BLUEBERRY-CORNMEAL MUFFINS

MAKES 12 MUFFINS

The crunch of cornmeal is a nice counterpoint to plump, tart blueberries in these muffins. You're probably not thinking about healthy food when you are about to eat a baked good, but these treats actually have some great qualities to boast about: Cornmeal is a source of whole grains and blueberries are bursting with antioxidants.

1 Preheat the oven to 400°F (200°C). Line 12 standard muffin cups with paper liners.

2 In a bowl, stir together the flour, brown sugar, cornmeal, baking powder, baking soda, salt, and nutmeg. In a large bowl, combine the eggs, milk, and melted butter. Using an electric mixer on low speed, beat the wet ingredients just until blended. Add the flour mixture and mix on low speed just until moistened. Switch to a wooden spoon and gently stir in the blueberries.

3 Spoon the batter into each muffin cup, filling it about three-fourths full. Mix the granulated sugar and cinnamon and sprinkle the mixture evenly over the tops. Bake until golden and a toothpick inserted into the center of a muffin comes out clean, 15–18 minutes.

4 Let the muffins cool in the pan on a wire rack for 2 minutes, then turn out onto the rack to cool a bit more. Serve warm.

{ INGREDIENTS DEMYSTIFIED: CORNMEAL
Cornmeal comes in all different hues and grind types. Fine-ground yellow or white cornmeal is the most basic variety and works in many dishes. Most types of cornmeal can be stored in an airtight container at room temperature for up to 1 year.

Unbleached all-purpose flour, 1½ cups (7½ oz/235 g)

Light brown sugar, ⅔ cup (5 oz/155 g) firmly packed

Fine-ground cornmeal, ½ cup (2½ oz/75 g)

Baking powder, 2 teaspoons

Baking soda, ½ teaspoon

Salt, ¼ teaspoon

Ground nutmeg, ¼ teaspoon

Eggs, 2

Whole milk, 1 cup (8 fl oz/250 ml)

Unsalted butter, 6 tablespoons (¾ stick/ 3 oz/90 g), melted

Fresh or frozen blueberries, 1 cup (4 oz/125 g)

Granulated sugar, 2 tablespoons

Ground cinnamon, 1 teaspoon

CHOCOLATE CHIP MUFFINS

MAKES 12 MUFFINS

Muffins don't get much better than this: mostly melted chocolate chips dotting a moist, rich, crumbly cake. The secret ingredient to making these muffins extra-tasty is the buttermilk, which lends a slight tang to the batter to help cut the chocolate chip muffin's inherent sweetness.

1 Preheat the oven to 350°F (180°C). Line 12 standard muffin cups with paper liners.

2 In a bowl, combine the buttermilk, melted butter, eggs, and vanilla. Using an electric mixer on low speed, beat until smooth. In a large bowl, stir together the flour, sugar, baking powder, baking soda, and salt. Make a well in the center of the flour mixture, then pour in the buttermilk mixture. Beat on low speed until smooth and well mixed, 1–2 minutes. Using a large rubber spatula, gently mix in the chocolate chips just until evenly distributed.

3 Spoon the batter into each muffin cup, filling it level with the rim of the cup. Bake until golden, dry, and springy to the touch, 20–25 minutes. A toothpick inserted into the center of a muffin should come out clean.

4 Let the muffins cool in the pan on a wire rack for 5 minutes, then turn onto the rack and let cool completely. Serve at room temperature.

Buttermilk, ¾ cup
(6 fl oz/180 ml)

Unsalted butter, ½ cup
(1 stick/4 oz/125 g), melted

Large eggs, 2

Vanilla extract, 1 tablespoon

Unbleached all-purpose
flour, 2 cups (10 oz/315 g)

Sugar, ¾ cup (6 oz/185 g)

Baking powder, 2 teaspoons

Baking soda, ½ teaspoon

Salt, ½ teaspoon

Semisweet chocolate chips,
2 cups (12 oz/375 g)

STRAWBERRY JAM MUFFINS

MAKES 12 MUFFINS

Who doesn't love spreading jam on fresh-out-of-the-oven baked goods? Now you can have your jam and eat it too—inside your muffins! At the center of these genius treats is a dollop of tangy jam, which bakes right along with them. In addition to the refreshing filling, sour cream contributes to a really moist crumb.

1 Preheat the oven to 375°F (190°C). Line 12 standard muffin cups with paper liners.

2 In a large bowl, stir together the flour, sugar, baking powder, baking soda, and salt. In another bowl, whisk together the sour cream, melted butter, eggs, and vanilla until smooth. Add the egg mixture to the flour mixture and stir just until evenly moistened. The batter will be slightly lumpy.

3 Spoon the batter into each muffin cup, filling it about one-third full. Drop a heaping teaspoonful of jam into the center of each muffin cup, then cover each with batter until level with the rim of the cup. Bake until golden, dry, and springy to the touch, 20–25 minutes.

4 Let the muffins cool in the pan on a wire rack for about 5 minutes, then turn onto the rack to cool a bit more. Serve the muffins warm or at room temperature.

Unbleached all-purpose flour, 2 cups (10 oz/315 g)

Sugar, ¾ cup (6 oz/185 g)

Baking powder, 1 tablespoon

Baking soda, ½ teaspoon

Salt, ½ teaspoon

Sour cream, 1¼ cups (10 oz/315 g)

Unsalted butter, 6 tablespoons (¾ stick/ 3 oz/90 g), melted

Large eggs, 2

Vanilla extract, 1 teaspoon

Seedless strawberry jam, ½ cup (5 oz/155 g)

{ **CHANGE IT UP: MUFFIN FILLINGS**
Any kind of jam will do in this recipe, not just strawberry. Try raspberry, apricot, or even fig. Fruit jams complement the sweetness of the muffin batter, but you could also go crazy with bacon, caramelized onion, or chile jam—but in those cases, we suggest omitting the vanilla.

TOMATO & GOAT CHEESE MUFFINS

MAKES 12 MUFFINS

Say hello to your new favorite savory muffin. Goat cheese works well alongside the tomatoes and herbs, but you can also make these with any type of creamy cheese; shredded mozzarella, crumbled queso fresco, and cream cheese work well too. Look for garbanzo flour where bulk baking or gluten-free ingredients are sold.

1 Preheat the oven to 400°F (200°C). Line 12 standard muffin cups with paper liners.

2 In a small frying pan over low heat, melt the butter. Add the green onions and sauté until almost translucent, 1–2 minutes. Stir in the basil. Remove from the heat and set aside.

3 In a large bowl, stir together the all-purpose and garbanzo flours, baking powder, and salt. In another bowl, whisk together the milk and eggs until blended. Make a well in the center of the flour mixture, then pour in the milk mixture and the butter mixture. Using a wooden spoon, stir just until evenly moistened, about 15–20 strokes. The batter will be thick and lumpy.

4 Spoon the batter into each muffin cup, filling it about half-full. Shape each piece of goat cheese into a round and set it in the center of each muffin batter. Place a few tomato pieces on top of the cheese and gently press into the batter. Cover the cheese and tomato with the remaining batter, dividing it evenly among the cups. Bake until golden, dry, and springy to the touch, 18–22 minutes. Do not overbake. To check the muffins for doneness, carefully lift a muffin from the pan; the sides should be browned.

5 Let the muffins cool in the pan on a wire rack for about 5 minutes, then turn onto the rack to let cool a bit more. Serve warm or at room temperature.

Unsalted butter, 6 tablespoons (¾ stick/ 3 oz/90 g)

Green onions, 4, finely chopped

Fresh basil, 2½ tablespoons minced

Unbleached all-purpose flour, 1½ cups (7½ oz/235 g)

Garbanzo flour, 1 cup (4½ oz/140 g)

Baking powder, 3½ teaspoons

Salt, ½ teaspoon

Whole milk, 1¼ cups (10 fl oz/310 ml)

Large eggs, 2

Soft goat cheese, 4 oz (125 g), cut into 12 pieces

Plum tomatoes, 2, chopped

DOUGHNUT MUFFINS

MAKES 9 MUFFINS

These muffins have the texture and flavor of buttermilk doughnuts, but they're baked instead of fried, so you don't need to worry about cleaning up the frying oil. You can even change up the toppings, if you like: Instead of cinnamon sugar, dip them into toasted coconut, chopped nuts, or even sprinkles.

1 Preheat the oven to 350°F (180°C). Butter 9 standard muffin cups; fill the unused cups one-third full with water to prevent the pan from warping.

2 To make the muffins, in a large bowl, using an electric mixer on medium speed, beat the butter and sugar until smooth, about 2 minutes. Add the egg and beat until smooth and blended. In another bowl, stir together the flour, baking powder, baking soda, salt, and nutmeg. Add the flour mixture to the butter mixture in 2 additions, alternating with the buttermilk and vanilla. Switch to a wooden spoon and stir just until evenly moistened. The batter will be slightly lumpy.

3 Spoon the batter into each muffin cup, filling it about three-fourths full. Bake until golden, dry, and springy to the touch, 20–25 minutes. A toothpick inserted into the center of a muffin should come out clean.

4 Let the muffins cool in the pan on a wire rack for about 5 minutes, then turn onto the rack to cool a bit more.

5 To make the topping, in a small, shallow bowl, stir together the sugar and cinnamon. Have ready the melted butter in another small bowl. Holding the bottom of a muffin, dip it into the melted butter, turning to coat it evenly. Immediately dip it into the cinnamon-sugar mixture, coating it evenly, then tap it to remove excess sugar. Transfer the coated muffin to the rack, right side up. Repeat with the remaining muffins. Let cool completely. Serve at room temperature.

FOR THE MUFFINS

Unsalted butter, 7 tablespoons (almost 1 stick/3½ oz/105 g), at room temperature, plus butter as needed

Sugar, ⅔ cup (5 oz/155 g)

Large egg, 1

Unbleached all-purpose flour, 1½ cups (7½ oz/235 g)

Baking powder, 1½ teaspoons

Baking soda, ½ teaspoon

Salt, ½ teaspoon

Ground nutmeg, ½ teaspoon

Buttermilk, ½ cup (4 fl oz/125 ml)

Vanilla extract, 1½ teaspoons

FOR THE TOPPING

Sugar, ⅔ cup (5 oz/155 g)

Ground cinnamon, 1 tablespoon

Unsalted butter, 6 tablespoons (¾ stick/ 3 oz/90 g), melted

LEMON LOAF

You could pay a few bucks for one slice of lemon bread at a coffee shop, or you can make a fresh, intensely lemony loaf at home for about the same price. Cutting a few slits into the warm loaf allows the sweet-and-sour glaze to seep deep into the pores of the bread, filling it with flavor.

1 Preheat the oven to 350°F (180°C). Lightly coat a 9-by-5-inch (23-by-13-cm) loaf pan with nonstick cooking spray.

2 In a large bowl, whisk together the flour, sugar, baking powder, baking soda, lemon zest, and salt until well mixed. In another bowl, whisk together the eggs, milk, oil, and vanilla until blended. Pour the egg mixture into the bowl with the flour mixture. Using a rubber spatula, mix until they are just combined, forming a thick, slightly lumpy batter. Pour the batter into the prepared pan, spreading it with the spatula to smooth the top. The pan will be about half full.

3 Bake the loaf until it is deeply browned with some golden cracks on top and it feels springy to the touch when pressed lightly in the middle, about 40 minutes. A butter knife inserted into the center should come out clean. Transfer the pan to a wire rack and insert the butter knife vertically into the cake in 8–10 uniformly spaced places. Set aside.

4 To make the glaze, in a small saucepan over medium-high heat, combine the sugar and lemon juice and bring to a boil. Continue to boil until the mixture is bubbling and frothy on the surface, about 3 minutes. Remove from the heat and immediately pour evenly over the surface of the hot loaf. Let the glazed loaf cool completely in the pan on the rack.

5 Run a thin knife around the inside edge of the pan to loosen the loaf. Carefully invert the loaf onto the rack and lift off the pan. Turn upright onto a serving plate, cut into slices, and serve.

FOR THE LOAF

Nonstick cooking spray

Unbleached all-purpose flour, 1½ cups (7½ oz/235 g)

Sugar, ¾ cup (6 oz/185 g)

Baking powder, 1 teaspoon

Baking soda, ¼ teaspoon

Lemon zest, finely grated from 1 large lemon

Salt, pinch

Large eggs, 2

Low-fat milk, ½ cup (4 fl oz/125 ml)

Canola oil, ¼ cup (2 fl oz/60 ml)

Vanilla extract, 1 teaspoon

FOR THE GLAZE

Sugar, ⅓ cup (3 oz/90 g)

Lemon juice, from 1 large lemon

CORN BREAD

Served warm with homemade chili, topped with a fried egg, or just with butter and honey, you can't go wrong with the classic comfort of corn bread. When shopping for cornmeal, keep in mind that the standard medium grind yields a relatively light-textured bread, while stone-ground cornmeal produces a more rustic quality.

1 Preheat the oven to 425°F (220°C). Generously butter an 8-inch (20-cm) square baking pan.

2 In a bowl, whisk together the cornmeal, flour, baking powder, baking soda, salt, and the corn kernels, if using. In a large bowl, using an electric mixer on medium speed, beat the eggs until blended. Add the honey, buttermilk, and oil and beat until blended. Add the flour mixture and beat on low speed just until mixed.

3 Pour the batter into the prepared pan and smooth the top with a rubber spatula. Bake until golden and a toothpick inserted into the center comes out clean, 20–25 minutes.

4 Let the bread cool slightly in the pan on a wire rack. Cut into 2-inch (5-cm) squares and serve warm.

Cornmeal, 1 cup (5 oz/155 g)

Unbleached all-purpose flour, 1 cup (5 oz/155 g)

Baking powder, 1½ teaspoons

Baking soda, ½ teaspoon

Salt, ½ teaspoon

Fresh corn kernels, from 3 ears (about 2 cups/ ¾ lb/375 g) (optional)

Large eggs, 2

Honey, 3 tablespoons

Buttermilk, 1⅓ cups (11 fl oz/340 ml)

Canola oil, 3 tablespoons

{ SPICE IT UP: PEPPER-CHEESE BREAD
Seed and chop 1 red bell pepper, then sauté it in 1 tablespoon olive oil until softened, about 3 minutes. Stir the sautéed pepper and ½ teaspoon ground cumin into the flour mixture. Proceed with the recipe. After 15 minutes of baking, sprinkle the top of the corn bread with ½ cup (2 oz/60 g) shredded pepper jack cheese.

BROWN SUGAR–SOUR CREAM BANANA BREAD

MAKES 2 LOAVES

Two loaves are better than one, especially with these intensely moist breads that use both mashed bananas and sour cream for optimum texture and flavor. Add dark chocolate chips to the batter for an indulgent treat. If you like, you can keep the extra loaf, wrapped tightly with foil, in the freezer for up to three months.

1 Preheat the oven to 350°F (180°C). Generously butter two 9-by-5-inch (23-by-13-cm) loaf pans.

2 In a bowl, sift together the flour, baking powder, baking soda, salt, cinnamon, and nutmeg. In a large bowl, whisk together the bananas, eggs, brown sugar, sour cream, vanilla, and melted butter. Add the flour mixture and whisk to combine.

3 Divide the batter between the prepared pans and sprinkle the tops with turbinado sugar. Bake until a toothpick inserted into the center of a loaf comes out clean, about 35 minutes.

4 Let the banana bread cool slightly in the pans and on a wire rack, then turn the loaves out onto a wire rack to cool completely before serving.

{ **BAKING WITH BANANAS** Baking with bananas is not only a great use for over-ripe fruit, but it's also a healthy way to bake, as bananas lend natural moistness, replacing heavy oils. Be sure to mash your bananas into a lump-free consistency, using a potato masher or a fork, to ensure a smooth texture to your baked goods.

Butter, for greasing

Unbleached all-purpose flour, 2 cups (10 oz/315 g)

Baking powder, 2 teaspoons

Baking soda, ½ teaspoon

Salt, ½ teaspoon

Ground cinnamon, ½ teaspoon

Ground nutmeg, ⅛ teaspoon

Extra-large, very ripe bananas, 3, smashed

Large eggs, 2

Dark brown sugar, 1 cup (7 oz/220 g) firmly packed

Sour cream, ½ cup (4 oz/125 g)

Vanilla extract, 1 teaspoon

Unsalted butter, ¼ cup (½ stick/2 oz/60 g), melted

Turbinado sugar, for sprinkling

ZUCCHINI BREAD

MAKES 3 MINI LOAVES OR 1 REGULAR LOAF

Zucchini bread is a retro-style treat, but once you pop a warm lightly buttered bite in your mouth, you won't care what century it's from. The prunes—actually dried plums—help provide moisture to the bread and help replace the need for a large amount of fat in the batter. If walnuts aren't your thing, go for pecans or almonds.

1 Preheat the oven to 350°F (180°C). Line three 6-by-3-inch (15-by-7.5-cm) loaf pans with parchment paper, cutting the short sides to fit, and cutting the long sides so that the parchment comes 2 inches (5 cm) up the sides of the pan. You can also use one 9-by-5-inch (23-by-13-cm) loaf pan.

2 Using a box grater-shredder, shred the zucchini using the large holes. In a bowl, using an electric mixer on medium speed, beat the sugar, oil, eggs, and vanilla until pale and creamy, about 1 minute. Switch to a wooden spoon and stir in the shredded zucchini until blended.

3 In a bowl, stir together the flour, baking powder, cinnamon, salt, baking soda, prunes, and walnuts. Add the flour mixture to the zucchini mixture and stir with the wooden spoon just until combined. The batter will be stiff. Scrape the batter into the prepared pan(s).

4 Bake until the bread is firm to the touch and pulls away from the pan sides, 35–40 minutes for small loaves or 50–60 minutes for a large loaf. A toothpick inserted into the center of a loaf should come out clean. Let the bread cool slightly in the pan(s) on a wire rack, then turn the loaves out onto a wire rack to cool completely before serving.

Zucchini, ½ lb (250 g), trimmed

Sugar, ¾ cup (6 oz/185 g)

Canola oil, ½ cup (4 fl oz/125 ml)

Large eggs, 2

Vanilla extract, 1 teaspoon

Unbleached all-purpose flour, 1½ cups (7½ oz/ 235 g), plus flour as needed

Baking powder, 2 teaspoons

Ground cinnamon, 1½ teaspoons

Salt, ½ teaspoon

Baking soda, ¼ teaspoon

Pitted moist-pack prunes, ½ cup (3 oz/90 g) chopped

Walnuts, ⅓ cup (1½ oz/45 g) coarsely chopped

{ **SWEETEN THEM UP** For an unconventional twist, add ¼ cup (¾ oz/20 g) unsweetened cocoa powder, sifted, to the flour mixture, or serve slices with honey and butter. Swirl the two condiments together or spread them on separately.

BISCUITS, SCONES & COBBLERS

ALL ABOUT
BISCUITS, SCONES & COBBLERS

Whether for breakfast, snack, a side dish, or desserts, these baked goods are endlessly versatile. They're perfect for fulfilling a sweet or a savory craving, since you can whip up batches in mere minutes.

Making biscuits, scones, and cobblers starts with a simple three-step process. First, the dry ingredients are mixed together. Then, butter is cut into the flour mixture, which helps create flaky layers during baking. Finally, a liquid, such as cream or buttermilk, is added to bring everything together. The butter pieces are suspended throughout the dough, which, when they come in contact with the heat of the oven,

> These baked goods all use a similar technique, which involves cutting cold butter into a flour mixture and then adding a liquid to bind the dough. The process creates rich, flaky layers when baked.

create tiny bursts of steam. The steam, fortified by the action of baking soda or baking powder, causes the dough to rise and creates flaky layers throughout the finished baked goods.

Tenderness is an important quality in biscuits, scones, and cobblers. To keep them light and airy, go easy on the mixing and handle the dough gently, especially after you add the liquid component to the dough; you don't want to develop the gluten in the flour, which could create a dense, tough texture.

WHY DO BAKING RECIPES CALL FOR UNSALTED BUTTER?

Many baking recipes call for unsalted butter for three reasons:

1   It tends to be fresher than salted butter
    (salt is used as a preservative).

2   It is low in moisture and has a sweet, delicate flavor.

3   You can better control the amount of salt that goes in a recipe.

But if you don't have unsalted butter on hand, go ahead and use salted butter. The recipes will still work fine, but you might want to cut down a bit on the salt in the recipe.

SECRETS TO SUCCESS

CHECK EXPIRATION DATES Be sure that your baking powder and baking soda are fresh—and don't even think about using that box in the back of the fridge! If in doubt, replace them.

NO BISCUIT CUTTER? No problem! A jar top or overturned glass can be used in place of a cutter.

KEEP IT COLD The success of biscuit-type doughs depends on the temperature of the many pieces of butter dispersed throughout the dough. Be sure your butter is very cold before adding it; room-temperature butter will not produce the desired texture.

USE A HOT OVEN In general, these types of baked goods use a hot oven—around 400°F (200°C) or higher. The high heat helps to quickly melt the butter pieces in the dough, creating flaky layers.

EMPLOY A LIGHT TOUCH The trick to making tender, flaky biscuits is minimal stirring and handling of the dough after you add any liquids.

FRUIT IN BAKED GOODS

Dry fruit works well for mixing into biscuit and scone batters, while fresh fruit is best for cobblers and crumbles. When planning a dish that bakes fresh fruit, opt for a firm but juicy variety. Try sturdy berries such as blueberries, blackberries, or raspberries (strawberries are challenging); stone fruit such as peaches, plums, or cherries; or firm tree fruits such as apples and pears. For the best results, look for what's in season.

MEDIUM MIXING BOWL

FORK

PASTRY BLENDER OR
TWO BUTTER KNIVES

ROLLING PIN

BISCUIT CUTTER

BAKING SHEET

WIRE COOLING RACK

HOW TO MAKE
BISCUITS & SCONES

1

MIX THE DRY INGREDIENTS
In a large bowl, using a fork, stir together the dry ingredients, such as flour, salt, and baking powder.

2

TOSS IN THE BUTTER
Add cold butter cubes to the flour mixture and toss well with a fork to coat the butter well.

3

CUT IN THE BUTTER
Using a pastry blender or two butter knives, cut the butter into the dry ingredients until the butter pieces are the size of small peas.

4

ADD THE COLD LIQUID
Add the liquid component
(usually milk or cream) and
stir with the fork just until
the ingredients are combined.

5

BRING IT ALL TOGETHER
Transfer the dough to a lightly
floured work surface. Using
a gentle touch, with your hands
or a rolling pin, pat the mixture
into a disk or rectangle.

6

CUT & BAKE
Using a biscuit cutter or a large
knife, cut the dough into the
desired shapes and bake.

BISCUIT BREAKFAST SANDWICHES

MAKES 12 BISCUITS

These savory sandwiches are a delicious contradiction: They're hearty and filling, yet somehow still dainty and cute. The basic baking powder biscuits are delectable on their own spread with butter and honey, but we suggest filling them up with your favorite breakfast ingredients. Better yet, load 'em up with all the fixings!

1 Preheat the oven to 425°F (220°C). Line a large rimmed baking sheet with parchment paper.

2 In a bowl, using a fork, stir together the flour, baking powder, and salt. Add the butter and toss it well to coat with the flour mixture. Using a pastry blender or 2 knives, cut in the butter just until the mixture forms coarse crumbs the size of small peas. Pour in the milk and mix with the fork just until the flour mixture is moistened and a loose dough is formed.

3 Turn the dough out of the bowl onto a lightly floured work surface and press it gently a few times until it clings together. Using a light touch or a lightly floured rolling pin, press or roll the dough into a rough square about ¾ inch (2 cm) thick. Using a long chef's knife, cut straight down and lift straight up to make 12 square biscuits. Place the biscuits on the prepared baking sheet, spacing them 1 inch (2.5 cm) apart. Bake until the biscuits are firm to the touch and golden-brown, 15–18 minutes.

4 Remove the biscuits from the oven and split them crosswise while still warm. Fill with your desired fillings, and serve right away.

FOR THE BISCUITS

Unbleached all-purpose flour, 2 cups (10 oz/315 g)

Baking powder, 2½ teaspoons

Salt, ½ teaspoon

Cold unsalted butter, 6 tablespoons (¾ stick/ 3 oz/90 g), cut into cubes

Whole milk, ¾ cup (6 fl oz/180 ml)

FOR THE FILLINGS

Scrambled eggs

Shredded Cheddar cheese

Cooked bacon, Canadian bacon, or prosciutto

Chopped green onions

Sliced avocado

Sliced tomato

{ **PARCHMENT PAPER: A KITCHEN WORKHORSE** Parchment paper provides a nonstick surface for baking pans, keeps baked food from sticking, and makes cleanup easy. It can withstand high oven temperatures, but should not be used for broiling or near an open flame. Look for it in the market next to the aluminum foil. Do not substitute waxed paper.

BUTTERMILK BISCUITS

MAKES 16 BISCUITS

There are few things more delicious and comforting than homemade
buttermilk biscuits. Flaky and rich, these particular ones get their signature
texture from the easy cutting method. Make sure your butter is cold,
mix with a light hand, and you'll have perfect, flaky-fluffy biscuits every time.

1 Preheat the oven to 425°F (220°C). Line a large rimmed baking
sheet with parchment paper.

2 In a bowl, using a fork, stir together the all-purpose and cake flours,
baking powder, sugar, salt, and baking soda. Add the butter and
toss it well to coat it with the flour mixture. Using a pastry blender
or 2 knives, cut in the butter just until the mixture forms coarse
crumbs the size of small peas. Pour in the buttermilk and mix
with the fork just until the flour mixture is moistened and a slightly
stiff, shaggy dough is formed.

3 Turn the dough out of the bowl onto a lightly floured work surface and
press it gently a few times until it clings together. Using a light touch
or a lightly floured rolling pin, press or roll the dough into a round
about 1 inch (2.5 cm) thick. Using a 3-inch (7.5-cm) biscuit cutter
dipped in flour, cut straight down and lift to punch out each biscuit.
Cut them as close together as possible for a minimum of scraps. Pack
the scraps together and reroll them to cut out more biscuits. You
should have about 16 biscuits.

4 Place the biscuits on the prepared baking sheet, spacing them about
1 inch (2.5 cm) apart. Bake until the biscuits are firm to the touch
and golden, 15–18 minutes.

5 Remove the biscuits from the oven and let them cool slightly on the
baking sheet. Serve warm.

Unbleached all-purpose
flour, 1½ cups (7½ oz/235 g)

Cake flour, 1½ cups
(6 oz/185 g), plus cake flour
as needed

Baking powder, 4 teaspoons

Sugar, 1 tablespoon

Salt, 1¼ teaspoons

Baking soda, ¼ teaspoon

Cold unsalted butter,
½ cup (1 stick/4 oz/125 g),
plus 2 tablespoons,
cut into chunks

Cold buttermilk,
1 cup (8 fl oz/250 ml)

CHEESE BISCUITS

MAKES 20 BISCUITS

For these savory biscuits, you can skip the usual rolling and shaping steps, because they are baked in muffin cups instead of a baking sheet. Make these round, cheesy bites to serve alongside comfort foods like pulled pork or chili, or put them out as a tempting (but deceptively easy) side dish for a brunch with friends.

1 Preheat the oven to 350°F (180°C). Have ready two 12-cup muffin pans. Butter 20 of the cups and fill the unused cups with water to prevent the pan from warping.

2 In a large bowl, using a fork, stir together the flour, baking powder, baking soda, and salt. Add the butter pieces and toss them well to coat with the flour mixture. Using a pastry blender or 2 knives, cut in the butter just until the mixture forms coarse crumbs the size of small peas. Add the cheese and mix with the fork just to combine. Add the egg and buttermilk, then switch to a wooden spoon and stir gently just until the dough forms a sticky mass. Stir a little more aggressively for about 10 seconds; the mass will form a moist, sticky clump on the spoon and will start to pull away from the sides of the bowl. The dough should be very soft.

3 Using a rubber spatula, scrape the dough from the bowl onto a lightly floured work surface. With floured hands, fold the dough over and gently knead it 6–8 times; it will remain sticky. Using a large knife or a bench scraper, cut the dough in half, then divide each half into 10 equal portions; don't worry if they are lumpy and uneven. Place each portion in a prepared muffin cup. Bake until the biscuits are firm to the touch and golden, 25–30 minutes.

4 Remove the biscuits from the oven and let cool slightly in the muffin pan, then turn the biscuits out onto wire racks. Serve warm.

Butter, for greasing

Unbleached all-purpose flour, 4 cups (20 oz/625 g), plus flour for sprinkling

Baking powder, 4 teaspoons

Baking soda, 1 teaspoon

Salt, 1½ teaspoons

Cold unsalted butter, ¾ cup (1½ sticks/6 oz/ 185 g), cut into pieces

Sharp Cheddar cheese, 2 cups (½ lb/250 g) shredded

Large egg, 1, lightly beaten

Cold buttermilk, 1¾ cups (14 fl oz/430 ml)

STRAWBERRY SHORTCAKES

MAKES 8 SERVINGS

Warm shortcakes, split and filled with whipped cream and sugared strawberries, are an old-school treat. These golden biscuits are dropped from a spoon instead of rolled and cut, which creates a jagged, crunchy crust after baking. Raspberries, blackberries, or sliced peaches can replace the strawberries, if you like.

1 Preheat the oven to 425°F (220°C). Line a large rimmed baking sheet with parchment paper.

2 In a bowl, using a fork, stir together the flour, granulated sugar, baking powder, and salt. Add the butter and toss it well to coat with the flour mixture. Using a pastry blender or 2 knives, cut in the butter just until the mixture forms large, coarse crumbs the size of small peas. In a small bowl, whisk together the egg and the ⅓ cup (3 fl oz/80 ml) cream until blended. Pour the egg mixture over the flour mixture and mix with a rubber spatula just until moistened. Add additional cream, 1 tablespoon at a time, as needed to form a soft dough that is wet enough to be dropped from a spoon.

3 Using a large spoon, drop the dough onto the prepared baking sheet in mounds about 3 inches (7.5 cm) wide and about ¾ inch (2 cm) high, spacing them 1 inch (2.5 cm) apart. You should have about 8 shortcakes. Brush the tops of the shortcakes with 1–2 tablespoons cream and sprinkle with the turbinado sugar. Bake until the shortcakes are firm to the touch and golden-brown, 12–15 minutes.

4 While the shortcakes are baking, prepare the filling. In a bowl, using a fork, crush 1 cup (4 oz/125 g) of the berries. Add the remaining berries and the granulated sugar, mix well, and set aside. Transfer the shortcakes from the baking sheet to a wire rack and let cool for 15 minutes.

5 To serve, split the warm shortcakes horizontally and place the bottom half of each, cut side up, on a plate. Spoon the berries on top, dividing them evenly. Top each with some whipped cream. Cover with the shortcake tops and serve right away.

FOR THE DOUGH

Unbleached all-purpose flour, 2 cups (10 oz/315 g)

Granulated sugar, ¼ cup (2 oz/60 g)

Baking powder, 1 tablespoon

Salt, ½ teaspoon

Cold unsalted butter, ½ cup (1 stick/4 oz/125 g), cut into ½-inch (12-mm) pieces

Large egg, 1

Heavy cream, ⅓ cup (3 fl oz/80 ml), plus heavy cream as needed

Turbinado sugar, 2 tablespoons

FOR THE FILLING

Strawberries, 2 pints (1 lb/500 g), hulled and sliced

Granulated sugar, 3 tablespoons

Whipped cream (page 115), for serving

CRANBERRY-APRICOT-ORANGE SCONES

MAKES 12 SCONES

The secret to tender scones is threefold: Handle them sparingly, using a light touch; work quickly; and bake them immediately after cutting. The optional glaze adds a sweet, elegant finish. Enjoy these classic British-style treats with all the traditional additions: butter, jam or lemon curd, crème fraîche, and warm cups of tea or coffee.

1 Preheat the oven to 425°F (220°C). Line a large rimmed baking sheet with parchment paper.

2 In a bowl, using a fork, stir together the flour, granulated sugar, baking powder, baking soda, salt, and orange zest. Add the butter and toss it well to coat with the flour mixture. Using a pastry blender or 2 knives, cut in the butter until the mixture forms coarse crumbs the size of small peas. Pour in the buttermilk and mix with the fork just until a sticky dough forms. Stir in the cranberries and apricots just until evenly distributed.

3 Scrape the sides and bottom of the bowl and turn the dough out onto a lightly floured work surface. With floured hands, fold the dough over and gently knead 8–10 times; the dough will be very soft. Press and pat the dough into a loose rectangle about 1½ inches (4 cm) thick. Using a large knife, divide the dough in half. Pat each portion into a round ¾ inch (2 cm) thick and 8 inches (20 cm) in diameter.

4 Cut each round pizza style, into 6 wedges. Place the wedges on the prepared baking sheet, spacing them 2 inches (5 cm) apart. Bake until golden, 14–18 minutes. Transfer the scones from the baking sheet to a wire rack to cool.

5 To make the glaze, if desired, in a small bowl, stir together the confectioners' sugar with the orange juice. Adjust the consistency with a little more juice, if needed; it should be thick but pourable. Brush or drizzle the glaze over the hot scones. Let stand for at least 10 minutes to set the glaze.

FOR THE SCONES

Unbleached all-purpose flour, 3 cups (15 oz/470 g), plus flour as needed

Granulated sugar, 3 tablespoons

Baking powder, 2½ teaspoons

Baking soda, ½ teaspoon

Salt, ½ teaspoon

Finely grated zest from 1 orange

Cold unsalted butter, 10 tablespoons (1¼ sticks/ 5 oz/155 g), cut into pieces

Cold buttermilk, 1 cup (8 fl oz/250 ml)

Dried cranberries, ¾ cup (3 oz/90 g)

Dried apricots, ¼ cup (1½ oz/45 g) chopped

FOR THE GLAZE (OPTIONAL)

Confectioners' sugar, ¾ cup (3 oz/90 g), sifted

Fresh orange juice, 1 tablespoon, or as needed

BACON & CHEESE SCONES

MAKES 12 SCONES

While most people think of scones as sweet treats, they can also be filled with savory ingredients, like these irresistible rounds of meat-and-cheese goodness, for a delicious change of pace. For a sinfully delicious treat, spread halved scones with sweet onion or bacon jam.

1 Preheat the oven to 400°F (200°C). Line a large rimmed baking sheet with parchment paper.

2 In a frying pan over medium heat, cook the bacon, stirring occasionally, until crisp, about 10 minutes. Using a slotted spoon, transfer the bacon to paper towels to drain.

3 In a large bowl, using a fork, stir together the flour, cheese, baking powder, pepper, and salt. Add the butter and toss it well to coat with the flour mixture. Using a pastry blender or two knives, cut in the butter until the mixture forms coarse crumbs the size of small peas. In a small bowl, whisk together the egg and cream until blended. Pour the egg mixture over the flour mixture and stir with the fork just until the dough comes together.

4 Turn the dough onto a lightly floured work surface. Sprinkle the bacon over the top and then use your hands to fold and push the dough to distribute the bacon. Bring the dough together into a ball. Using a floured rolling pin, roll out the dough into a round about ½ inch (12 mm) thick. Using a 3-inch (7.5-cm) biscuit cutter, cut out as many scones as you can. Pack the scraps together and reroll them to cut out more scones. You should have about 12 scones. Space the scones evenly on the prepared baking sheet. Bake until the scones are golden-brown, about 12 minutes.

5 Transfer the scones from the baking sheet to a wire rack to cool slightly. Serve warm.

Applewood-smoked bacon, 3 thick slices, cut crosswise into ½-inch (12-mm) pieces

Unbleached all-purpose flour, 2 cups (10 oz/315 g)

Parmesan cheese, 1 cup (4 oz/125 g) grated

Baking powder, 2 teaspoons

Freshly ground pepper, ½ teaspoon

Salt, pinch

Cold unsalted butter, ½ cup (1 stick/4 oz/125 g), cut into chunks

Large egg, 1

Heavy cream or whole milk, ¾ cup (6 fl oz/180 ml)

LEMON CREAM SCONES

These scones have a flaky, slightly cakelike texture and are very rich, thanks to a heavy dose of cream in the dough. The lemon flavor is layered in three ways: lemon zest and lemon juice are mixed into the dough, and a lemony-sugary glaze is brushed on after baking.

1 Preheat the oven to 400°F (200°C). Line a large rimmed baking sheet with parchment paper.

2 In a large bowl, using a fork, stir together the granulated sugar and lemon zest. Sift the flour, baking powder, and salt into the bowl and stir together. Add the butter and toss it well to coat with the flour mixture. Using a pastry blender or 2 knives, cut in the butter until the mixture forms coarse crumbs the size of small peas. Pour the ¾ cup (6 fl oz/180 ml) cream and the ¼ cup (2 fl oz/60 ml) lemon juice over the flour mixture and stir with the fork just until the dough comes together. The dough will be thick, but moist.

3 Turn the dough out onto a lightly floured work surface and gently press into a round about ¾ inch (2 cm) thick. Using a large knife, cut the round, pizza style, into 8 wedges. Place the wedges on the prepared baking sheet, spacing them evenly apart. Brush the rounds lightly with cream. Bake until golden, 15–17 minutes.

4 Transfer the scones from the baking sheet to a wire rack to cool slightly. While the scones are cooling, in a small bowl, stir together the confectioners' sugar and the remaining 2 teaspoons lemon juice. Adjust the consistency with a little more juice, if needed; it should be thick but pourable. Brush or drizzle the glaze over the hot scones. Let stand for at least 1 minutes to set the glaze. Serve warm.

Granulated sugar, 3 tablespoons

Lemon zest, finely grated from 2 lemons

Unbleached all-purpose flour, 2 cups (10 oz/315 g)

Baking powder, 2 teaspoons

Salt, ¼ teaspoon

Cold unsalted butter, ½ cup (1 stick/4 oz/125 g), cut into chunks

Heavy cream, ¾ cup (6 fl oz/180 ml), plus heavy cream as needed

Lemon juice, ¼ cup (2 fl oz/60 ml) plus 2 teaspoons

Confectioners' sugar, ¼ cup (1 oz/30 g), sifted

PEACH COBBLER

MAKES 8 SERVINGS

Peach cobbler is always a hit. With its biscuitlike topping, the cobbler celebrates fruit of all kinds. But no amount of sugar will improve the flavor of lackluster fruits, so wait for your favorite type of fragrant, in-season stone fruits or berries for the best results. A scoop of vanilla ice cream makes this good thing even better.

1 Preheat the oven to 375°F (190°C). Lightly butter a 9-by-13-inch (23-by-33-cm) cake pan or baking dish.

2 In a bowl, toss together the peaches, brown sugar, and cornstarch. Spread the mixture in the prepared dish and bake for 15 minutes.

3 In a bowl, using a fork, stir together the flour, the ¼ cup (2 oz/60 g) granulated sugar, baking powder, and salt. Add the butter and toss it well to coat with the flour mixture. Using a pastry blender or 2 knives, cut in the butter until the mixture forms coarse crumbs the size of small peas. In another bowl, whisk together the half-and-half, egg, and vanilla. Pour the half-and-half mixture over the flour mixture and stir with the fork just until the dough comes together.

4 Drop the dough onto the filling in 8 heaping spoonfuls. Bake until the peach filling is bubbling, the topping is golden-brown, and a toothpick inserted into the topping comes out clean, 30–40 minutes more.

5 Transfer the cobbler to a wire rack and let cool for at least 30 minutes. Serve warm.

{ PREP WORK: PEELING PEACHES
If your peaches are excessively fuzzy, peeling them will improve their texture. Using a paring knife, cut a small X in the bottom of each peach. Working with a few at a time, plunge the peaches into boiling water just until the skins loosen, about 30 seconds. Using a slotted spoon, transfer them to a bowl of ice water. Use the knife to peel the peach skins from the fruit, starting at the X.

Butter for greasing

Peaches, 5 lb (2.5 kg), pitted and sliced

Light brown sugar, ½ cup (3½ oz/105 g) firmly packed

Cornstarch, 2 tablespoons

Unbleached all-purpose flour, 2 cups (10 oz/315 g)

Granulated sugar, ¼ cup (2 oz/60 g), plus sugar as needed

Baking powder, 1 tablespoon

Salt, ½ teaspoon

Cold unsalted butter, 6 tablespoons (¾ stick/3 oz/90 g), cut into chunks

Half-and-half, ¾ cup (6 fl oz/180 ml)

Large egg, 1

Vanilla extract, 1 teaspoon

THREE-BERRY COBBLERS

MAKES 6 SERVINGS

You can use any kind or combination of fresh berries here. This recipe makes individual cobblers, which are perfect for dinner parties, but you can also make one big cobbler in a 9-inch (23-cm) baking pan or dish and serve it family-style, right at the table with a large spoon. Bake the large one for about 45 minutes.

1   Preheat the oven to 375°F (190°C). Lightly butter 6 shallow 1-cup (250-ml) ramekins or baking dishes.

2   To make the filling, in a large bowl, gently toss the berries with the sugar, flour, zest, and salt. Pour the mixture into the prepared ramekins, dividing evenly, and set aside.

3   To make the topping, in a bowl, using a fork, stir together the flour, sugar, baking powder, cinnamon, and salt in a bowl. In another bowl, whisk together the egg, buttermilk, melted butter, and vanilla until well blended. Pour the buttermilk mixture over the flour mixture and, using a silicone spatula, fold gently until the flour is moistened and the mixture forms a soft dough.

4   Drop the dough onto the fruit in large spoonfuls. The topping will not completely cover the fruit. Bake until the fruit filling is bubbling, the topping is golden-brown, and a toothpick inserted into the topping comes out clean, about 30 minutes.

5   Remove the cobblers from the oven and let stand on a wire rack for a few minutes to cool. Serve warm or at room temperature.

{ FANCY FOOD TERM: COBBLER   A cobbler is any kind of dessert baked in a dish with a fruit filling and biscuit or piecrust top. A drop biscuit cobbler is one of the easiest varieties, as you simply drop pieces of biscuit on top of fruit and let it bake into a golden-brown crust.

FOR THE FILLING

Butter, for greasing

Mixed berries, such as blackberries, raspberries, and blueberries, 3 pints (1½ lb/750 g)

Sugar, ⅓ cup (3 oz/90 g)

Unbleached all-purpose flour, 1 tablespoon

Finely grated lemon zest, 1 teaspoon

Salt, pinch

FOR THE TOPPING

Unbleached all-purpose flour, 1¼ cups (6½ oz/200 g)

Sugar, ⅓ cup (3 oz/90 g)

Baking powder, 2 teaspoons

Ground cinnamon, ½ teaspoon

Salt, ¼ teaspoon

Large egg, 1, at room temperature

Buttermilk, ½ cup (4 fl oz/125 ml)

Unsalted butter, 6 tablespoons (¾ stick/ 3 oz/90 g), melted

Vanilla extract, ½ teaspoon

APPLE CRUMBLE

MAKES 6 SERVINGS

This homey dessert doesn't really fit the biscuits-and-cobbler mold, but it
seemed remiss not to include a simple, delicious crumble in an easy baking book.
Since most of the ingredients are pantry staples, this is a perfect anytime dessert.
Or if you're feeling decadent, leftover crumble makes a delicious breakfast.

1 Preheat the oven to 375°F (190°C). Butter a small rectangular baking dish. Peel, core, and slice the apples, then put them into a bowl. Add the lemon juice and granulated sugar and toss to coat. Place the apples in the prepared dish in an even layer.

2 In a bowl, stir together the oats, brown sugar, flour, cinnamon, salt, and walnuts, if using. Drizzle the melted butter over the oat mixture and toss with a fork until evenly moistened. Cover the apples evenly with the oat mixture.

3 Bake until the apples are tender and the topping is golden-brown, 35–45 minutes. Keep an eye on the crumble as it bakes; if the topping begins to brown before the apples are fully cooked, cover the pan with foil and reduce the oven temperature to 350°F (180°C).

4 Let the crumble cool slightly in the pan on a wire rack. Spoon the crumble into bowls, pour some cream over the top, if desired, and serve warm.

{ FANCY FOOD TERM: CRUMBLE A crumble is a baked dessert with a crumbly topping consisting of oats, flour, butter, and sometimes nuts. Any kind of non-citrus fruit can serve as the base of a crumble, such as apples, pears, stone fruits, or berries.

Butter for greasing

Large Granny Smith apples, 2 lb (1 kg)

Fresh lemon juice, 1 tablespoon

Granulated sugar, 2 tablespoons

Rolled oats, ¾ cup (2½ oz/75 g)

Light brown sugar, ½ cup (3½ oz/105 g) firmly packed

Unbleached all-purpose flour, ⅓ cup (2 oz/60 g)

Ground cinnamon, 1 teaspoon

Salt, pinch

Walnuts, ½ cup (2 oz/90 g) chopped (optional)

Unsalted butter, 6 tablespoons (¾ stick/ 3 oz/90 g), melted

Heavy cream, for serving (optional)

PIES

ALL ABOUT
PIES

Pie dough can be used for so much more than just a sweet holiday dessert with a flaky crust. Filled with a savory egg mixture, it transforms a few basic ingredients into a versatile quiche. Sandwiched around berries and formed into small pockets, the dough makes a novel handheld dessert. Atop a bubbling mixture of creamy chicken and vegetables, it tops a classic comforting chicken stew. The possibilities are endless with pie dough, and, as a bonus, it's supereasy to make.

There are three key elements to remember when working with pie dough: Keep the dough cool, work with a well-floured surface and rolling pin, and use a light touch so you don't overwork the dough.

First, keep the dough cool by making sure the butter and water are very cold when blending it into the dough. Next, be sure to roll out the dough on a clean work surface that's been lightly but thoroughly coated with flour. You want just enough to keep the dough from sticking, but not so much that it changes the consistency of the dough. Finally, use a light touch throughout the dough-making process—you want to avoid developing the gluten in the flour. Roll out the dough just to the thickness and size you need. Keeping the dough cool, preventing it from sticking, and handling it minimally will keep your dough rich and flaky.

WHAT DOES "BLIND BAKING" MEAN?

Blind baking is a term for baking a piecrust before it's filled. The rolled-out crust is first fitted into a pie pan. Then, the crust is lined with foil and filled with pie weights. Next, the crust is baked, either partially or fully, and the weights work to keep the crust smooth and shapely as it bakes. After baking, the foil and weights are removed to make room for the filling.

ASSORTED MIXING BOWLS

FORK

PASTRY BLENDER OR
TWO BUTTER KNIVES

ROLLING PIN

PIE PAN OR BAKING SHEET

PIE WEIGHTS

SILICONE SPATULA,
WOODEN SPOON, OR WHISK

SECRETS TO SUCCESS

NIX OVERBROWNING
If your piecrusts are browning too much before the filling is done, cut about 3 strips of foil and use them to carefully cover the edges, leaving the filling in the center exposed.

HARD-TO-BUDGE DOUGH If your dough is too cold to roll out, let it stand at room temperature for 10–20 minutes to soften it slightly.

SHUT THE FRONT (OVEN) DOOR
Resist the urge to open the oven to check on a baking pie. Every time the door is opened, the oven temperature is altered and the action could affect the outcome of the finished pie.

SUBSTITUTE PIE WEIGHTS If you don't have pie weights on hand in your kitchen, use dried beans or uncooked rice. You can save the beans or rice for future baking needs—just don't plan to cook them for a meal!

FOOD PROCESSOR PIE DOUGH If you have a food processor, you can use it to quickly make pie dough. Pulse together the dry ingredients. Add the butter and pulse 8–10 times to form pea-sized crumbs. Add the ice water and pulse 10–12 times just until the dough comes together in a mass, but does not form a ball.

FANCY FLUTED PIECRUSTS

Fork tines pressed around the border of a piecrust add an easy crimped design, but you can take the presentation up a notch by creating a simple fluted edge with your fingers. Hold the thumb and index finger of one hand 1 inch (2.5 cm) apart and press them inward at the outer edge of the pastry rim while pressing your other index finger outward from the inside edge of the pastry rim. Repeat the pattern as you progress in intervals around the pan.

HOW TO HANDLE
PIE DOUGH

1
PREPARE TO ROLL
Unwrap the dough and put it on
a lightly floured work surface.
Lightly dust the top of the dough
and a rolling pin with flour.

2
ROLL AWAY
Starting at the center and
working outward, roll the
dough into a round that is
about 2 inches (5 cm) larger
than the pie pan (or according
to the recipe). As you work,
lift and turn the dough,
and re-dust it with flour, if
necessary, to prevent sticking.

3
MOVE THE DOUGH TO THE PAN
Carefully roll the dough around the
rolling pin, position it over the pie pan
or baking sheet, and unroll the dough.

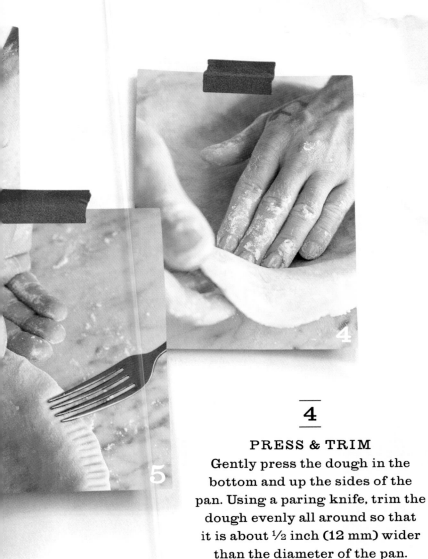

HOW TO MAKE
PIE DOUGH

To make the pie dough, follow the instructions below. For a double batch of dough, simply multiply the ingredients by 2.

Unbleached all-purpose flour, 1⅓ cups (7 oz/220 g)

Salt, ¼ teaspoon

Cold unsalted butter, ½ cup (1 stick/4 oz/125 g), cut into cubes

Ice water, 4 tablespoons (2 fl oz/60 ml), plus more if needed

In a bowl, combine the flour and salt and stir with a fork. Add the butter cubes and toss with the fork to coat well with the flour. Using a pastry blender or 2 knives, cut in the butter until the mixture forms large, coarse crumbs the size of small peas. Drizzle the ice water over the flour-butter mixture and toss with a fork until the dough is evenly moist. If the dough seems too crumbly, add more ice water, a tablespoon at a time, and toss to mix.

When the dough is done, it should come together in a rough mass. Gather the dough together gently and form into a disk. Wrap the disk in plastic wrap and refrigerate for at least 30 minutes before using.

4
PRESS & TRIM
Gently press the dough in the bottom and up the sides of the pan. Using a paring knife, trim the dough evenly all around so that it is about ½ inch (12 mm) wider than the diameter of the pan.

5
GIVE IT A FANCY EDGE
Fold the edge of the dough under itself so that it is even with the pan sides. Press the tines of a fork all around to form a decorative edge.

BANANA CREAM PIE

If you want to make a friend for life or impress your pals at a dinner party,
bake them this irresistible pie. The creamy, vanilla-scented custard,
buttery crust, and rich whipped cream topping show off sweet
banana slices in a heavenly dessert that just screams, "Share me!"

1 Follow the instructions on page 78 to line a 9-inch (23-cm) pie pan
with the rolled-out dough and form a decorative edge. Freeze the
dough-lined pan for 30 minutes. Meanwhile, preheat the oven to
425°F (220°C).

2 Line the frozen crust with foil and fill with pie weights. Bake for
15 minutes. Remove the foil and weights and continue to bake until
the crust is golden, 4–5 minutes longer. Let the crust cool completely
on a wire rack. Reduce the oven temperature to 325°F (165°C).

3 In a small bowl, whisk together ½ cup (4 fl oz/125 ml) of the milk and
the cornstarch. In a heatproof bowl, beat the yolks until blended.

4 In a saucepan, combine the remaining 2½ cups (20 fl oz/625 ml)
milk, the sugar, and salt. Place over medium heat and bring to a
simmer, stirring to dissolve the sugar. Gradually whisk the hot milk
mixture into the egg mixture, then return to the saucepan. Heat over
medium heat until the mixture comes to a boil, whisking constantly.
Reduce the heat to low and let bubble for 30 seconds. Remove from
the heat and whisk in the butter and vanilla. Strain through a medium-
mesh sieve into a heatproof bowl. Press a piece of plastic wrap
directly onto the surface of the filling, and pierce the plastic a few
times with a knife to allow the steam to escape. Place the bowl
in a larger bowl of ice water and let cool until lukewarm.

5 Spread the banana slices in the crust. Spread the filling on top.
Press a piece of plastic wrap directly on the surface of the filling and
refrigerate until chilled, at least 1 hour. Remove the plastic wrap.
Swirl the whipped cream over the filling. Cut into 8 wedges and serve.

**Pie Dough (page 79), rolled
into a 12-inch (30-cm) round**

**Whole milk, 3 cups
(24 fl oz/750 ml)**

**Cornstarch, ⅓ cup
(1 oz/40 g)**

Large egg yolks, 4

Sugar, ⅔ cup (5 oz/155 g)

Salt, ⅛ teaspoon

**Unsalted butter, 2 tablespoons,
cut into pieces**

Vanilla extract, 1 teaspoon

**Large bananas, 2, peeled
and thinly sliced**

**Whipped cream (page 115),
for serving**

PUMPKIN PIE

MAKES 10 SERVINGS

You don't need to wait around until Thanksgiving for an excuse to make
a pumpkin pie. Pumpkin purée is available in most stores year-round.
And if you think about it, pumpkin pie is made from a squash that's high in
vitamins and minerals, so eating a slice can only be good for you, right?

1 Follow the instructions on page 78 to line a 9-inch (23-cm) pie pan
with the rolled-out dough and form a decorative edge. Freeze the
dough-lined pan for 30 minutes. Meanwhile, preheat the oven to
425°F (220°C).

2 Line the frozen crust with foil and fill with pie weights. Bake for
15 minutes. Remove the foil and weights and continue to bake until
the crust is golden, 4–5 minutes longer. Let the crust cool completely
on a wire rack. Reduce the oven temperature to 325°F (165°C).

3 In a large bowl, combine the pumpkin purée, cream, brown sugar,
eggs and egg yolk, flour, vanilla, cinnamon, nutmeg, cloves, and
salt and whisk until smooth. Pour into the crust.

4 Bake the pie until the filling is set but the center just barely jiggles,
50–60 minutes. Let cool completely on a wire rack.

5 Cut into 10 wedges. Serve at room temperature or slightly chilled,
topping with whipped cream, if desired.

Pie Dough (page 79), rolled
into a 12-inch (30-cm) round

Pumpkin purée, 1 can
(15 oz/470 g)

Heavy cream, 1 cup
(8 fl oz/250 ml)

Light brown sugar, ⅔ cup
(5 oz/155 g) firmly packed

Whole large eggs, 2, plus
1 large egg yolk, at room
temperature

Unbleached all-purpose
flour, 4 teaspoons

Vanilla extract, 1 teaspoon

Ground cinnamon,
½ teaspoon

Ground nutmeg, ¼ teaspoon

Ground cloves, pinch

Salt, pinch

Whipped cream (page 115),
for serving (optional)

MAPLE-PECAN PIE

MAKES 8 SERVINGS

Gooey and melt-in-your-mouth delicious, pecan pie is an easy favorite. This one is flavored with maple syrup, which gives it a homey taste. If you're a pecan pie fanatic, keep pecans and pie dough in the freezer for the next time a pie urge strikes. You'll want to use real maple syrup here, as the artificial stuff will taste, well, artificial.

1 Follow the instructions on page 78 to line a 9-inch (23-cm) pie pan with the rolled-out dough and form a decorative edge. Freeze the dough-lined pan for 30 minutes. Meanwhile, preheat the oven to 425°F (220°C).

2 Line the frozen crust with foil and fill with pie weights. Bake for 15 minutes. Remove the foil and weights and continue to bake until the crust is golden, 4–5 minutes longer. Let the crust cool completely on a wire rack. Reduce the oven temperature to 325°F (165°C).

3 In a saucepan over medium-high heat, boil the maple syrup for 8–10 minutes (this will concentrate its flavor and texture). Remove from the heat and pour the syrup into a heatproof measuring pitcher. The syrup should be reduced to 1½ cups (16½ oz/515 g). If necessary, return the syrup to the saucepan and continue to boil until sufficiently reduced. Let cool to room temperature before proceeding.

4 In a bowl, stir together the reduced maple syrup, eggs, brown sugar, melted butter, vanilla, and salt until well mixed. Add the pecans and stir well. Pour into the crust, making sure the pecans are evenly distributed.

5 Bake the pie until the center is slightly puffed and firm to the touch, 30–35 minutes. Let cool on a wire rack until just slightly warm, about 45 minutes. Cut into wedges and serve warm.

Pie Dough (page 79), rolled into a 12-inch (30-cm) round

Maple syrup, 2 cups (22 oz/690 g)

Large eggs, 2, lightly beaten

Light or dark brown sugar, ¼ cup (2 oz/60 g) firmly packed

Unsalted butter, 2 tablespoons, melted

Vanilla extract, 1 teaspoon

Salt, ⅛ teaspoon

Pecans, 1½ cups (6 oz/185 g) coarsely chopped

PLUM-ALMOND CROSTATA

MAKES 6-8 SERVINGS

A crostata is what the Italians call a galette, or flat pie. You don't need a pie pan to make one, just a baking sheet and parchment paper. This rustic dessert comes together in a few basic steps. The key to success is to use slightly firm plums and cut the wedges as uniformly as possible, so they cook evenly.

1 Line a large baking sheet with parchment paper. Carefully transfer the rolled-out dough to the prepared baking sheet and refrigerate to keep it cold. Meanwhile, in a bowl, toss together the plums, granulated sugar, flour, and salt.

2 Remove the dough from the refrigerator and scatter the almond paste pieces evenly over the center of the dough round, leaving a 2-inch (5-cm) border of dough. Using a slotted spoon, distribute the plum mixture evenly over the almond paste, again leaving the border uncovered. Reserve any juices in the bowl. Fold the dough edges over the plums, loosely pleating the dough and leaving the crostata open in the center. Using a pastry brush, brush the dough with the egg white and sprinkle with turbinado sugar. Drizzle any reserved juices from the bowl over the plums. Dot the plums with the butter. Refrigerate on the baking sheet for 30 minutes. Meanwhile, preheat the oven to 400°F (200°C).

3 Bake the crostata until the crust is golden and the juices bubble in the center, about 40 minutes.

4 Let the crostata cool slightly on the baking sheet on a wire rack. Cut into wedges and serve warm.

Pie Dough (page 79), rolled into a 14-inch (35-cm) round

Firm but ripe plums, 1¼ lb (625 g), pitted and cut into wedges ½ inch (12 mm) thick

Granulated sugar, ¼ cup (2 oz/60 g)

Unbleached all-purpose flour, 2 teaspoons

Salt, pinch

Almond paste, ¼ lb (125 g), broken into ½-inch (12-mm) pieces

Large egg white, 1, lightly beaten

Turbinado sugar, 2 tablespoons

Unsalted butter, 1 tablespoon, cut into small pieces

{ PREP WORK: WORKING WITH STUBBORN STONE FRUIT When working with fruit that doesn't separate easily from the pit, you'll need to cut off the flesh in halves, positioning the knife close to either side of the pit. Then, cut the halves into wedges.

APPLE GALETTE WITH SALTED CARAMEL SAUCE

MAKES 6–8 SERVINGS

We love making fruit galettes. Instead of fitting the piecrust into a pie pan, the rolled-out dough is put directly on a baking sheet. The filling gets piled right on top, and the dough is pleated, free-form, around the filling to enclose it. This apple galette comes with a tempting rum-soaked caramel sauce.

1 Line a baking sheet with parchment paper. Carefully transfer the rolled-out dough to the prepared baking sheet and refrigerate to keep it cold. Meanwhile, in a bowl, toss together the apple slices, ⅓ cup (3 oz/90 g) of the granulated sugar, the lemon zest, lemon juice, cinnamon, and salt.

2 Remove the dough from the refrigerator and arrange the apple mixture in the center of the dough round, leaving a 2-inch (5-cm) border of dough. Fold the dough edges over the apples, loosely pleating the dough and leaving the galette open in the center. In a bowl, whisk the egg with 1 tablespoon of the water. Using a pastry brush, brush the dough with the egg mixture and sprinkle with the turbinado sugar. Cut 1 tablespoon of the butter into small pieces and scatter over the apples. Refrigerate on the baking sheet for 30 minutes. Meanwhile, preheat the oven to 400°F (200°C).

3 Bake the galette until the crust is deeply browned, about 40 minutes. Let cool on the baking sheet on a wire rack.

4 Meanwhile, in a tall, heavy saucepan, combine the remaining 1 cup (8 oz/250 g) granulated sugar and 1 tablespoon water. Cover and bring to a simmer over medium heat, checking often. Once the sugar starts to melt, uncover and swirl the pan occasionally until the sugar is dissolved, about 5 minutes. Continue to simmer until the sugar turns a deep amber-brown, 3–5 minutes longer. Remove from the heat, carefully add the cream (the caramel will hiss and bubble vigorously), and whisk until smooth. Whisk in the remaining 1 tablespoon butter, the rum, and coarse salt. Let cool slightly. To serve, cut the galette into wedges and drizzle with the sauce. Serve at room temperature.

Pie Dough (page 79), rolled into a 14-inch (35-cm) round

Crispin or Pink Lady apples, 3, peeled, cored, and cut into ¼-inch (6-mm) slices

Granulated sugar, 1⅓ cups (11 oz/340 g)

Lemon zest, finely grated from 1 lemon

Lemon juice, 1 tablespoon

Ground cinnamon, ½ teaspoon

Salt, pinch

Large egg, 1

Water, 2 tablespoons

Turbinado sugar, 2 tablespoons

Unsalted butter, 2 tablespoons

Heavy cream, ½ cup (4 fl oz/125 ml)

Dark rum, 3 tablespoons

Coarse sea salt, ½ teaspoon

QUICHE LORRAINE

MAKES 6–8 SERVINGS

Filled with a creamy egg custard, mixed with melted Gruyère cheese, and dotted with nuggets of meaty bacon, this is the quintessential French quiche. Serve it for breakfast with a fruit salad, or for lunch—or even dinner—with a green salad on the side. Seek out thick-sliced bacon, which will lend a meatier bite than thin-sliced.

1 Follow the instructions on page 78 to line a 9-inch (23-cm) pie pan with the rolled-out dough and form a decorative edge. Freeze the dough-lined pan for 30 minutes. Meanwhile, preheat the oven to 425°F (220°C).

2 Line the frozen crust with foil and fill with pie weights. Bake for 15 minutes. Remove the foil and weights and continue to bake until the crust is golden, 4–5 minutes longer. Let the crust cool completely on a wire rack. Reduce the oven temperature to 375°F (190°C).

3 In a frying pan over medium heat, cook the bacon, stirring occasionally, until crisp, about 10 minutes. Using a slotted spoon, transfer the bacon to paper towels.

4 In a bowl, whisk together the eggs, milk, cream, nutmeg, and a pinch each of salt and pepper. Stir in the bacon and cheese. Pour into the crust. Bake the quiche until golden on top and just barely jiggling in the center, 45–50 minutes.

5 Let the quiche cool on a wire rack for at least 20 minutes. Cut into wedges and serve warm or at room temperature.

Pie Dough (page 79), rolled into a 12-inch (30-cm) round

Thick-sliced bacon, ¾ lb (375 g), cut crosswise into ½-inch (12-mm) pieces

Large eggs, 6

Whole milk, 1½ cups (12 fl oz/375 ml)

Heavy cream, 1½ cups (12 fl oz/375 ml)

Nutmeg, ⅛ teaspoon freshly grated

Salt and freshly ground pepper

Gruyère cheese, 1 cup (4 oz/125 g), coarsely grated

BROCCOLI-CHEDDAR QUICHE

MAKES 8 SERVINGS

Like a frittata, a quiche is superversatile because you can add whatever ingredients sound good to you. Broccoli and Cheddar is a popular vegetarian combo, but you can also toss in some cooked, cubed ham, sliced red bell pepper, or even swap the Cheddar for pepper jack. Enjoy this protein-filled dish for any meal, or as a snack.

1 Follow the instructions on page 78 to line a 9-inch (23-cm) pie pan with the rolled-out dough and form a decorative edge. Freeze the dough-lined pan for 30 minutes. Meanwhile, preheat the oven to 425°F (220°C).

2 Line the frozen crust with foil and fill with pie weights. Bake for 15 minutes. Remove the foil and weights and continue to bake until the crust is golden, 4–5 minutes longer. Let the crust cool completely on a wire rack. Reduce the oven temperature to 350°F (180°C).

3 Bring a medium saucepan three-fourths full of lightly salted water to a boil over high heat. Add the broccoli and cook until the florets are barely tender, about 5 minutes. Drain well and pat dry with kitchen towels. In a bowl, whisk together the half-and-half, eggs, dill, ½ teaspoon salt, and ¼ teaspoon pepper until combined. Stir in the cheese. Pour the mixture into the crust. Bake the quiche until golden on top and just barely jiggling in the center, about 35 minutes.

4 Let the quiche cool on a wire rack for at least 20 minutes. Cut into wedges and serve warm or at room temperature.

Pie Dough (page 79), rolled into a 12-inch (30-cm) round

Broccoli florets, 2 cups (4 oz/125 g)

Half-and-half, 2 cups (16 fl oz/500 ml)

Large eggs, 4

Fresh dill, 1 tablespoon minced

Salt and freshly ground pepper

Sharp Cheddar cheese, 1 cup (4 oz/125 g) shredded

BUTTERMILK PIE

This take on custard pie uses buttermilk instead of regular milk or cream, which gives it a fresh, tangy taste. Buttermilk pie is a classic Southern dish and its old-timey charm is making its way back to today's bakeshop menus. In our version, plump fresh raspberries lend flavor and color for modern tastes.

1 Follow the instructions on page 78 to line a 9-inch (23-cm) pie pan with the rolled-out dough and form a decorative edge. Freeze the dough-lined pan for 30 minutes. Meanwhile, preheat the oven to 425°F (220°C).

2 Line the frozen crust with foil and fill with pie weights. Bake for 15 minutes. Remove the foil and weights and continue to bake until the crust is golden, 4–5 minutes longer. Let the crust cool completely on a wire rack. Reduce the oven temperature to 350°F (180°C).

3 In a bowl, using an electric mixer on medium speed, beat the butter and granulated and brown sugars until smooth and creamy, about 3 minutes. Beat in the eggs. Add the flour, salt, buttermilk, vanilla, and lemon zest and mix with a wooden spoon just until incorporated. Pour into the crust.

4 Bake the pie until golden on top and just barely jiggling in the center, about 45 minutes. Let the pie cool completely on a wire rack.

5 Pile the raspberries on top and dust with confectioners' sugar, if you like. Cut into 8 wedges and serve at room temperature.

Pie Dough (page 79), rolled into a 12-inch (30-cm) round

Unsalted butter, ½ cup (1 stick/4 oz/125 g), at room temperature

Granulated sugar, 1 cup (8 oz/250 g)

Light brown sugar, ¼ cup (2 oz/60 g) firmly packed

Large eggs, 3, lightly beaten

Unbleached all-purpose flour, 2 tablespoons

Salt, pinch

Buttermilk, 1 cup (8 fl oz/250 ml)

Vanilla extract, 1½ teaspoons

Lemon zest, ½ teaspoon finely grated

Raspberries, 1 pint (8 oz/250 g)

Confectioners' sugar, for sprinkling (optional)

BLACKBERRY MINI PIES

MAKES 6 MINI PIES

No one can resist a pocket-sized pie bursting with vibrant, juicy berries. You'll be tempted to eat them out of hand, until the sweet purple juice spills out onto your shirt. Better yet, serve them on a plate alongside a scoop of vanilla ice cream. Other sturdy varieties of berries, such as blueberries or raspberries, also work well in this recipe.

1 Using a 4-inch (10-cm) round cookie cutter, cut out 3 or 4 rounds from each rolled-out dough round. Pack the scraps together and reroll them to cut out more rounds. You should have 12 rounds.

2 Line a baking sheet with parchment paper. In a bowl, toss together the blackberries, sugar, cornstarch, and salt. Transfer 6 of the dough rounds to the prepared baking sheet. Arrange the blackberries evenly over the dough rounds, leaving a small border of dough uncovered. Using a small pastry brush, brush the border with cold water. Lay the remaining dough rounds over the blackberries, centering them as best you can. Gently press the top of each dough round down over the berries. With the tines of a fork, press the outer edge of the 2 dough rounds together.

3 Refrigerate the mini pies on the baking sheet until the dough is firm, 15–20 minutes. Meanwhile, preheat the oven to 375°F (190°C).

4 Bake until the mini pies are golden, 35–40 minutes. Let the pies cool slightly on the baking sheet on a wire rack. Serve warm.

Double batch of Pie Dough (page 79) rolled into 2 rounds, each ⅛ inch (3 mm) thick

Blackberries, 1 pint (8 oz/250 g)

Sugar, 3 tablespoons

Cornstarch, 2 tablespoons

Salt, pinch

Cold water, for brushing

{ MIX IT UP: EXPERIMENTING WITH SIZES
Although these adorable little pies are perfect single servings, sometimes you just want a little less or a little more. With the same ingredients, you can make twelve 2-inch (5-cm) pies for bite-sized treats, or three 8-inch (20-cm) pies for large, shareable servings.

CHICKEN POT PIE

MAKES 6 SERVINGS

These savory pies are easier to make than they look, thus perfect for impressing friends. Both the pastry and the filling can be made ahead and refrigerated for up to 8 hours before assembly. Use leftover chicken or grab a rotisserie chicken from the store, let it cool slightly, pull off the skin, and shred the meat with your fingers.

1 In a large frying pan over medium heat, melt 1 tablespoon of the butter. Add the mushrooms and cook, stirring occasionally, until they begin to brown, about 6 minutes. Stir in the onion and carrots, cover, and cook, stirring occasionally, until the onion is tender, about 5 minutes. Remove from the heat and stir in the peas.

2 In a large saucepan, melt the remaining 5 tablespoons (2½ oz/ 75 g) butter over medium-low heat. Whisk in the flour and let it bubble gently for 1 minute. Gradually whisk in the broth and wine and then the tarragon. Bring to a boil, whisking frequently. Stir in the shredded chicken and the vegetable mixture and season to taste with salt and pepper. Let cool in the pan until lukewarm, about 1 hour.

3 Preheat the oven to 400°F (200°C). Spoon the chicken mixture into six 1½-cup (12-fl oz/375-ml) ovenproof ramekins.

4 Place the dough on a lightly floured work surface and dust the top with flour. Roll it out into a large rectangle about ⅛ inch (3 mm) thick. Using a 6-inch (15-cm) saucer as a template, use a knife to cut out 6 dough rounds. Beat the egg with a pinch of salt. Lightly brush each round with the egg. Place 1 round, egg side down, over each ramekin, keeping the pastry taut and pressing it around the ramekin edges to adhere. Place the ramekins on a rimmed baking sheet. Lightly brush the tops with more egg.

5 Bake until the pastry is puffed and golden, about 25 minutes. Transfer each ramekin to a dinner plate and serve. Be careful, as the filling will be very hot!

Unsalted butter, 6 tablespoons (¾ stick/ 3 oz/90 g)

Button mushrooms, ½ lb (250 g), quartered

Small yellow onion, 1, chopped

Carrots, ½ cup (1½ oz/ 75 g) finely diced

Fresh frozen peas, ⅓ cup (1½ oz/45 g)

Unbleached all-purpose flour, ⅓ cup (2 oz/60 g) plus 1 tablespoon, plus flour for dusting

Chicken broth, 4½ cups (36 fl oz/1.1 l)

White wine, ⅓ cup (3 fl oz/80ml)

Fresh tarragon, 2 teaspoons minced

Cooked, shredded chicken, 4 cups (1½ lb/750 g)

Salt and freshly ground pepper

Double batch of Pie Dough (page 79)

Large egg, 1

CAKES & CUPCAKES

ALL ABOUT
CAKES &
CUPCAKES

From coffee dates and birthday parties, to after-dinner desserts and miniature pick-me-ups, cakes—in all their various shapes, sizes, and flavors—tempt any sweet tooth. The cakes within this chapter are flavored with real ingredients, like fresh lemon juice and fruits, vanilla extract, honey, and rum—no boxed mixes allowed!

A successful cake is the result of quality ingredients, a properly prepared pan, a carefully made batter, and serving it at the perfect temperature for optimum flavor and texture.

Following a few simple tips can really elevate your cake from ordinary to extraordinary. First, take the time to preheat the oven thoroughly and prepare the pan as directed in the recipe (spray with cooking spray, rub with butter, line with parchment), both of which help cakes bake evenly and slide out of the pans with ease. Next, take care when mixing cake batters to mix the batter in stages, and use a light hand when the flour is incorporated, which ensures an airy batter and tender crumb. Finally, cool the cake according to the instructions in the recipe—sometimes partially, sometimes fully—before removing it from the pan, to ensure maximum enjoyment. With these tips in mind, cake making is almost as easy as opening a boxed mix, but a hundred times more rewarding and delicious.

WHAT DOES "FOLDING" MEAN?

When combining two mixtures of different consistencies, folding helps blend them without deflating the batter. Using a silicone spatula, pile half of the lighter mixture (e.g., whipped cream or egg whites) onto the denser mixture. With the spatula, slice down through the center of both mixtures and pull it toward the edge of the bowl, then up the side and over the lighter mixture. Continue this motion, rotating the bowl a quarter turn and repeating the process until the two mixtures are incorporated.

ASSORTED MIXING BOWLS

ELECTRIC MIXER OR WHISK

SILICONE SPATULA

CAKE PAN

SKEWER OR TOOTHPICK

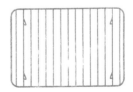

WIRE COOLING RACK

SECRETS TO SUCCESS

SPOON & SWEEP
To ensure consistent results every time, use the spoon-and-sweep method for measuring dry ingredients: Use a spoon to fill a dry measuring cup full to overflowing with the ingredient, such as flour, then level it off with the back of a butter knife.

EASY DECORATING
If you don't have the inclination to make a separate frosting or topping, dust cakes with confectioners' sugar poured through a fine-mesh sieve.

SQUAT & PEEK
Liquids are best measured in a clear glass or plastic measuring pitcher with a spout for pouring. Place the pitcher on a flat work surface and pour in the liquid. Squat down so you can read the measurement at eye level.

TAKE THE CAKE To remove a cake from the pan, run a thin knife along the inside edge of the pan. Keep the knife firm against the pan so you don't cut into the cake. Then, place a wire rack on top of the cake, and holding the cake and rack together, invert them and set the rack on the work surface. Lift off the cake pan.

BAKING ASSURANCE
To ensure even baking, especially when you are making more than one item at a time, rotate the pans 180 degrees about halfway through the baking time. You can also switch the pan positions on the racks, if desired.

ROOM TEMPERATURE IS BEST
Many cake recipes call for butter and eggs to be at room temperature before beginning. There is a good reason for this: Butter is easier to work with when in its softened state, and eggs disperse more easily in the batter, creating a more evenly cooked cake. Set aside 15–30 minutes to bring ingredients to room temperature before you start the batter.

HOW TO MAKE
CAKES

1

PREPARE THE PANS

To line a pan with parchment, trace its shape on a sheet of parchment paper and cut to fit. Instead, you can also butter and flour the pans (see page 103).

2

CREAM BUTTER & SUGAR

Using an electric mixer on medium speed, beat together room-temperature butter and sugar until light and creamy, about 2 minutes.

3

ALTERNATE TO FINISH THE BATTER

Beat in the eggs, then beat in the dry ingredients and liquid ingredients alternately, just until the batter is combined.

4

SCRAPE & BAKE
Scrape the batter into the pan,
smoothing the top with
a silicone spatula, then put
in a preheated oven.

5

TEST FOR DONENESS
Insert a skewer or toothpick into the
center of the cake. If it comes out
clean, the cake is done. If not, bake
for a few more minutes and test again.

6

COOL COMPLETELY
Place the cake pan on a
wire rack to cool completely
before unmolding.

RASPBERRY–SOUR CREAM CRUMB CAKE

MAKES 8 SERVINGS

In this irresistible cake, the flavors come in three tempting tiers: buttery vanilla cake on the bottom, tangy fresh raspberries in the middle, and a crumbly lemon-scented layer on the top. The best part is, once the cake is in the oven, your work is done—no whipping or frosting required!

1 Preheat the oven to 350°F (180°C). Butter and flour a 10-inch (25-cm) round cake pan.

2 To make the topping, in a small bowl, using a fork, stir together the flour, sugar, and lemon zest. Add the melted butter and stir until the mixture is crumbly. Set aside.

3 To make the cake, in a large bowl, stir together the flour, sugar, baking powder, baking soda, and salt. In another bowl, using an electric mixer on low speed, beat the eggs, sour cream, and vanilla until well blended. Make a well in the center of the flour mixture and add the sour cream mixture. Beat on medium speed until smooth and fluffy, about 2 minutes. Using a silicone spatula, scrape the batter into the prepared pan and spread evenly. Cover evenly with the raspberries. Sprinkle the crumb topping evenly over the berries. Bake until the topping is golden and a toothpick inserted into the center of the cake comes out clean, about 40 minutes.

4 Transfer the pan to a wire rack and let cool for 20 minutes. Cut into 8 wedges and serve warm or at room temperature.

> { **HOW TO: BUTTERING & FLOURING BAKING PANS** Some recipes call for buttering and flouring pans to help keep cakes from sticking while baking. First, rub the inside part of the pan all over with a thin coating of butter. Next, dust the pan with all-purpose flour, turning it around so that the flour coats the entire buttered surface. Finally, tap the pan to remove any excess flour.

FOR THE CRUMB TOPPING

Unbleached all-purpose flour, 1 cup (5 oz/155 g)

Granulated sugar, ⅔ cup (5 oz/155 g)

Lemon zest, finely grated from 1 lemon

Unsalted butter, ½ cup (1 stick/4 oz/125 g), melted

FOR THE CAKE

Unbleached all-purpose flour, 1¾ cups (9 oz/280 g)

Granulated sugar, 1 cup (8 oz/250 g)

Baking powder, 2 teaspoons

Baking soda, ¼ teaspoon

Salt, ¼ teaspoon

Large eggs, 3

Sour cream, 1 cup (8 oz/250 g)

Vanilla extract, 1 teaspoon

Fresh raspberries, 1 pint (8 oz/250 g)

LEMON PUDDING CAKE

We refer to this tangy treat as "magic cake," because it is really two desserts in one. The bottom layer is a dense pudding and the top layer is a light-and-airy cake. After you make the batter and put it in the pan, some magical kind of alchemy happens in the heat of the oven to separate the batter into two divinely delicious elements.

1 In a large, clean bowl, using an electric mixer on medium speed, beat the egg whites and cream of tartar until foamy. Raise the speed to medium-high and beat just until soft peaks form (slightly bent tips when the beater is lifted). Slowly add ¼ cup (2 oz/60 g) of the sugar while you continue to beat until stiff, glossy peaks form (pointed tips that stand firm and straight on the beater). Set aside.

2 Preheat the oven to 350°F (180°C). Have ready a deep 9-inch (23-cm) pie pan.

3 In a bowl, whisk together the milk, cream, and egg yolks until blended. Whisk in the lemon zest, lemon juice, and melted butter. In a large bowl, stir together the flour, salt, and the remaining ¼ cup (2 oz/60 g) sugar. Pour in the milk mixture and whisk until smoothly blended. Using a rubber spatula, gently fold in one-half of the egg whites until almost incorporated. Add the remaining egg whites and gently fold until just combined. Pour into the pie pan. Bake until the top feels firm and the center is just slightly jiggly, about 35 minutes. Let cool in the pan on a wire rack. Cut into 8 wedges and serve warm.

Large eggs, 3, separated

Cream of tartar, ¼ teaspoon

Sugar, ½ cup (4 oz/125 g)

Whole milk, 1 cup (8 fl oz/250 ml)

Heavy cream, ½ cup (4 fl oz/125 ml)

Lemon zest, 1 tablespoon grated

Fresh lemon juice, ¼ cup (2 fl oz/60 ml)

Unsalted butter, 3 tablespoons, melted

Unbleached all-purpose flour, ¼ cup (1½ oz/45 g)

Salt, ⅛ teaspoon

{ **PREP WORK: SEPARATING AN EGG**
Have ready 3 clean bowls. Crack the egg, hold it over a bowl, and carefully pull the shell apart. Transfer the yolk back and forth from one shell half to the other, letting the egg white fall into the bowl below. Drop the yolk into the second bowl. If the egg separates cleanly, pour the white into the third bowl. To avoid getting any yolk into your whites, break each new egg over the first empty bowl and transfer the whites each time.

PINEAPPLE UPSIDE-DOWN CAKE

MAKES 8-10 SERVINGS

This retro-cool cake has timeless appeal. The dark rum and pineapple flavors are reminiscent of a piña colada. Buttermilk lends a slight tang to offset the sweetness. When the cake is inverted, the fruit topping is baked right in, so there's no need for a separate frosting. Look for fresh pineapple at a salad bar or natural foods store.

1 Preheat the oven to 350°F (180°C). Have ready a 9-inch (23-cm) round cake pan. In a sauté pan over medium heat, melt the 2 tablespoons butter. Add ½ cup (4 oz/125 g) of the sugar and cook, stirring occasionally, until the sugar melts and turns light brown, 5–7 minutes. Add the pineapple and cook, without stirring, until the pineapple releases its juice and the sugar is a medium caramel color, about 5 minutes. Pour the mixture into the cake pan, using a silicone spatula to get every last bit. Spread the mixture evenly in the pan.

2 Sift the flour, baking powder, and salt into a bowl. In a large bowl, using an electric mixer on medium speed, beat the ½ cup (1 stick/ 4 oz/125 g) butter with the remaining ¾ cup (6 oz/190 g) sugar until the mixture is pale and creamy, about 2 minutes. Slowly pour in the eggs, beating until incorporated. Add the flour mixture in 3 additions, alternating with the buttermilk in 2 additions, beating on medium-low speed just until combined. Beat in the rum. Pour the batter on top of the pineapple and spread it evenly to the edge of the pan. Bake until the top is browned, 30–40 minutes. Let cool in the pan on a wire rack for 10 minutes.

3 Run a table knife around the edge of the pan and shake it to make sure the cake is not sticking to the bottom. (If it is, set the pan on the stove top over low heat and heat for 1–2 minutes, gently shaking the pan until the cake is free.) Place a serving platter upside down on the pan. Wearing oven mitts, invert the platter and pan. Lift off the pan. Dislodge any pineapple pieces that stick to the pan and arrange on top of the cake. Cut into wedges and serve at room temperature.

Unsalted butter, ½ cup (1 stick/4 oz/125 g) plus 2 tablespoons, at room temperature

Sugar, 1¼ cups (10 oz/315 g)

Fresh pineapple chunks, 2 cups (12 oz/375 g)

Unbleached all-purpose flour, 1½ cups (7½ oz/235 g)

Baking powder, 1½ teaspoons

Salt, ¼ teaspoon

Large eggs, 2, at room temperature, lightly beaten

Buttermilk, ¾ cup (6 fl oz/180 ml), at room temperature

Dark rum, 1 tablespoon

COCONUT POUND CAKE WITH MANGO-LIME TOPPING

MAKES 8-10 SERVINGS

The tempting coconut flavor in this easy pound cake is reinforced by coconut extract. Since it's baked in a loaf pan and is easy to slice, it makes a great cake to have around for snacking. Look for fresh mango cubes in a salad bar, produce section of a supermarket, or natural foods store.

1 Position a rack in the lower third of the oven and preheat to 325°F (165°C). Lightly spray a 9-by-5-inch (23-by-13-cm) loaf pan with cooking spray. Dust the pan with flour, then tap out any excess.

2 Spread the coconut on a rimmed baking sheet and toast in the oven, stirring occasionally, until lightly golden, about 5 minutes. Set aside. Sift the flour, baking powder, and salt into a bowl and set aside. Using an electric mixer on medium speed, beat the butter and ¾ cup (6 oz/185 g) sugar until smooth, about 2 minutes. Add the eggs one at a time, beating well after each addition. Add the coconut and vanilla extracts. Beat in half of the flour mixture, then half of the milk, and repeat to add the remaining flour and milk. Reserve 1 tablespoon of the shredded coconut for garnish and stir in the remainder. Scrape the batter into the prepared pan. Bake until the top is golden and the center is firm to the touch, 55–60 minutes.

3 Let the cake cool in the pan on a wire rack for 20–30 minutes, then turn it out of the pan onto the rack to cool.

4 In a bowl, mix the mango cubes with the lime juice and the remaining 1–2 tablespoons sugar to taste. Cut the cake into slices and top with the mango mixture. Garnish with the reserved coconut and lime zest, if using.

Nonstick cooking spray

Unbleached all-purpose flour, 1½ cups (7½ oz/235 g) plus flour for dusting

Sweetened shredded coconut, 1 cup (4 oz/125 g)

Baking powder, 1½ teaspoons

Salt, ½ teaspoon

Unsalted butter, ½ cup (1 stick/4 oz/125 g), at room temperature

Sugar, ¾ cup (6 oz/185 g) plus 1–2 tablespoons

Large eggs, 2

Coconut extract, 1½ teaspoons

Vanilla extract, ½ teaspoon

Whole milk, ½ cup (4 fl oz/125 ml)

Fresh mango cubes, 2 cups (12 oz/375 g)

Fresh lime juice, 2 teaspoons

Lime zest, grated, for garnish (optional)

CLASSIC YELLOW CAKE WITH CHOCOLATE FROSTING

MAKES 10-12 SERVINGS

Everyone should have a classic cake recipe in their repertoire, and this moist yellow version is just the ticket. Like the boxed variety, it's simple and delicious, yet infinitely better. Covered in a smooth chocolate frosting, this cake is fit for any occasion: birthdays, celebrations, dinner parties, or just a perfect ending to a great dinner.

1 Preheat the oven to 350°F (180°C). Line the bottoms of two 9-inch (2-cm) round cake pans with parchment paper.

2 Sift the flour, baking powder, and salt into a bowl. In a small bowl, combine the milk and vanilla. In a large bowl, using an electric mixer on medium speed, beat the butter and sugar until pale and creamy, about 2 minutes. Slowly pour in the eggs, beating until incorporated. Add the flour mixture in 3 additions, alternating with the milk mixture in 2 additions, beating on medium-low speed just until combined.

3 Divide the batter among the prepared pans and spread it evenly. Bake until the cakes are puffed and a toothpick inserted into the centers comes out clean, 20–25 minutes. Let the cakes cool completely on a wire rack.

4 To make the frosting, put the chocolate in a heatproof bowl. Microwave on low for 1 minute. Stir and continue to microwave on low in 30-second bursts, stirring in between intervals, until the chocolate is melted and smooth. Let cool to lukewarm, about 5 minutes. In a large bowl, using an electric mixer on medium speed, beat the butter and confectioners' sugar until well blended, about 1 minute. Beat in the vanilla. Beat in the chocolate, then the cream, until the mixture is fluffy, about 1 minute.

5 Run a table knife around the edges of the pans. Invert one cake onto a plate, and peel off the parchment. Using a long, thin metal spatula, frost the cake with a thick layer of frosting. Invert the other cake top side down on the first layer. Frost the top of the cake. If desired, frost the sides of the cake, too. Refrigerate for about 30 minutes to set the frosting. Cut into wedges and serve at room temperature.

FOR THE CAKE

Unbleached all-purpose flour, 2 cups (10 oz/315 g)

Baking powder, 2 teaspoons

Salt, ¼ teaspoon

Whole milk, ½ cup (4 fl oz/125 ml), at room temperature

Vanilla extract, 2 teaspoons

Unsalted butter, 1 cup (8 oz/225 g), at room temperature

Sugar, 1½ cups (12 oz/375 g)

Large eggs, 4, at room temperature, lightly beaten

FOR THE FROSTING

Unsweetened chocolate, 2 oz (60 g), chopped

Unsalted butter, ½ cup (1 stick/4 oz/125 g), at room temperature

Confectioners' sugar, 1 cup (4 oz/125 g), sifted

Vanilla extract, 1 teaspoon

Heavy cream, 1 tablespoon

RED VELVET CUPCAKES

MAKES 12 CUPCAKES

Arguably the most popular flavor at any modern cupcake shop, red velvet is a tempting mix of cocoa-flavored cake, tangy cream cheese frosting, and a unique color palette. In the old days, beets in the batter contributed to the cakes' vibrant red hue. Today, it's easier to use a few drops of red food coloring to achieve the iconic look.

1 Preheat the oven to 350°F (180°C). Line 12 standard muffin cups with paper liners.

2 Sift the cake flour, cocoa powder, baking powder, and salt into a bowl. In a small bowl, whisk together the buttermilk, vanilla, vinegar, and red food coloring. In another bowl, using an electric mixer on medium-high speed, beat the sugar and butter until pale and creamy, about 2 minutes. Beat in the egg. Add the flour mixture in 3 additions, alternating with the buttermilk mixture in 2 additions, beating on low speed until combined and scraping down the sides of the bowl as needed.

3 Spoon the batter into each muffin cup, filling it about three-fourths full. Bake until a toothpick inserted into the center of a cupcake comes out clean, 20–22 minutes. Let the cupcakes cool in the pan on a wire rack for about 5 minutes, then turn out onto the rack to cool completely, about 1 hour.

4 Meanwhile, follow the instructions on page 112 to make the frosting. Frost the cupcakes and serve right away.

Cake flour, 1¼ cups (5 oz/155 g)

Unsweetened cocoa powder, 2 tablespoons

Baking powder, ¾ teaspoon

Salt, ¼ teaspoon

Buttermilk, ½ cup (4 fl oz/125 ml)

Vanilla extract, 1 teaspoon

White vinegar, ½ teaspoon

Red food coloring, 4 drops

Sugar, ¾ cup (6 oz/185 g)

Unsalted butter, 4 tablespoons (2 oz/60 g), at room temperature

Large egg, 1, at room temperature

Cream Cheese Frosting (page 112)

{ **FANCY FOOD TERM: CAKE FLOUR**
Cake flour, as opposed to all-purpose, is a fine-textured, soft wheat flour that has a silky feel in your hands. Its high starch content helps make cakes and pastries tender, and not chewy.

CARROT CUPCAKES

Allow yourself to be fooled into thinking the presence of vegetables in cupcakes makes them healthy, and these sweet treats will taste all the more enjoyable! Carrots add moistness, a natural orange hue, and an appealing texture to these cupcakes. Here, they're topped with fluffy whipped cream cheese frosting for a classic pairing.

1 Preheat the oven to 350°F (180°C). Line 12 standard muffin cups with paper or foil liners.

2 In a bowl, whisk together the flour, baking powder, baking soda, salt, and cinnamon. In another bowl, whisk together the carrots, sugar, oil, eggs, buttermilk, and vanilla. Using a rubber spatula, gently mix the flour mixture into the carrot mixture until completely combined.

3 Spoon the batter into each muffin cup, filling it about two-thirds full. Bake until golden and a toothpick inserted in the center of a cupcake comes out clean, 20–25 minutes. Let the cupcakes cool in the pan on a wire rack for 5 minutes, then turn out onto the rack to cool completely, about 1 hour.

4 Meanwhile, make the frosting: In a bowl, using an electric mixer on medium-high speed, beat the cream cheese, butter, and vanilla together until pale and creamy, about 2 minutes. Gradually beat in the confectioners' sugar until blended. Use right away, or if the consistency is too soft, refrigerate until the frosting is spreadable, about 15 minutes.

5 Using a long, thin metal spatula or a table knife, frost the cupcakes and serve right away.

{ INGREDIENT DEMYSTIFIED: CONFECTIONERS' SUGAR Confectioners' sugar is another word for powdered sugar. It's actually granulated sugar that's been crushed into a fine powder, which helps it blend easily into creamy mixtures and frostings.

Unbleached all-purpose flour, 1½ cups (7½ oz/235 g)

Baking powder, 1 teaspoon

Baking soda, ½ teaspoon

Salt, ½ teaspoon

Ground cinnamon, ½ teaspoon

Carrots, 1½ cups (7½ oz/ 235 g) finely grated

Granulated sugar, 1 cup (8 oz/250 g)

Vegetable oil, ¾ cup (6 fl oz/180 ml)

Large eggs, 2, at room temperature

Buttermilk, ¼ cup (2 fl oz/60 ml)

Vanilla extract, ½ teaspoon

FOR THE CREAM CHEESE FROSTING

Cream cheese, ¾ lb (375 g), at room temperature

Unsalted butter, 6 tablespoons (¾ stick/ 3 oz/90 g), at room temperature

Vanilla extract, ½ teaspoon

Confectioners' sugar, 1 cup (4 oz/125 g), sifted

HONEY & CHAI CUPCAKES

MAKES 12 CUPCAKES

If you love chai tea lattes, these are the cupcakes for you. Aromatic tea infuses the batter with hints of cardamom, cinnamon, cloves, ginger, and nutmeg. A light honey whipped cream is spread on top of the rich cakes in lieu of frosting, which makes these treats seem all the more like edible versions of the popular coffeehouse drink.

1 Preheat the oven to 350°F (180°C). Line 12 standard muffin cups with paper liners. In a small bowl, steep the tea bags in the boiling water for 5 minutes. Discard the tea bags and let the tea cool to room temperature.

2 In a bowl, whisk together the flour, brown sugar, baking soda, and salt. In a large bowl, combine the honey, melted butter, buttermilk, and egg. Add the flour mixture and, using an electric mixer on medium speed, beat until just combined, about 2 minutes. Add the cooled tea and beat until just combined, scraping down the sides of the bowl as needed.

3 Spoon the batter into each muffin cup, filling it about three-fourths full. Bake until a toothpick inserted in the center of a cupcake comes out clean, 18–20 minutes. Let the cupcakes cool in the pan on a wire rack for 5 minutes, then turn out onto the rack to cool completely, about 1 hour.

4 Meanwhile, make the honey whipped cream: In a chilled bowl, combine the cream and honey. Using an electric mixer on low speed, beat until slightly thickened, 1–2 minutes. Gradually increase the speed to medium-high and continue to beat until the cream holds soft peaks (slightly bent tips when the beater is lifted), 2–3 minutes.

5 Using a long, thin metal spatula or a table knife, frost the cupcakes with the honey whipped cream and serve right away.

Chai-spice tea bags, 3

Boiling water, ⅔ cup
(5 fl oz/150 ml)

Unbleached all-purpose
flour, 1¼ cups (6½ oz/
200 g)

Light brown sugar, ¾ cup
(6 oz/185 g) firmly packed

Baking soda, 1 teaspoon

Salt, ¼ teaspoon

Honey, ¼ cup (3 oz/90 g)

Unsalted butter,
4 tablespoons (½ stick/
2 oz/60 g), melted

Buttermilk, ¼ cup
(2 fl oz/60 ml)

Large egg, 1, at room
temperature

**FOR THE HONEY
WHIPPED CREAM**

Cold heavy cream, 1 cup
(8 fl oz/250 ml)

Honey, 2 tablespoons

TRES LECHES MINI CAKES

MAKES 12 MINI CAKES

Tres leches, literally "three milks" in Spanish, gets its name from the extra-creamy trio of sweetened condensed, evaporated, and whole milk used to soak the cakes. These mini versions of the traditional Mexican dessert pack all the milky sweetness plus a little dark rum into personal-sized cakes for a decidedly adult treat.

1 Preheat the oven to 350°F (180°C). Lightly spray 12 standard muffin cups with cooking spray.

2 In a large rectangular baking dish, stir together the sweetened condensed milk, evaporated milk, heavy cream, and rum. In a bowl, whisk together the flour, sugar, baking powder, and salt. Add the eggs, milk, and vanilla, whisking vigorously to combine. Spoon the batter into each muffin cup, filling it about two-thirds full. Bake until lightly golden and a toothpick inserted in the center of a cake comes out clean, 18–20 minutes. Transfer the pan to a wire rack.

3 While the cakes are still hot in the pan, pierce the top of each cake several times with a skewer. Carefully remove the cakes from the pan and place in the dish with the sweetened milk mixture. Spoon the milk mixture generously over each cake. Let the soaked cakes cool completely in the dish, about 1 hour. Transfer the cakes to an airtight container and chill for at least 4 hours or for up to 3 days, spooning more of the milk mixture over them from time to time.

4 When ready to serve, let the cupcakes stand at room temperature for about 10 minutes. Meanwhile, make the whipped cream: In a chilled bowl, combine the cream and sugar. Using an electric mixer on low speed, beat until slightly thickened, 1–2 minutes. Gradually increase the speed to medium-high and continue to beat until the cream holds soft peaks (slightly bent tips when a beater is lifted), 2–3 minutes.

5 Put the cakes in individual bowls and spoon some of the soaking liquid on top. Top each with whipped cream and serve right away.

Nonstick cooking spray

Sweetened condensed milk, 1 can (12 oz/375 g)

Evaporated milk, 1 can (12 oz/375 g)

Heavy cream, 1 cup (8 fl oz/250 ml)

Dark rum, ¼ cup (2 fl oz/60 ml)

Unbleached all-purpose flour, 1 cup (5 oz/155 g)

Sugar, ¾ cup (6 oz/185 g)

Baking powder, 1 teaspoon

Salt, ¼ teaspoon

Large eggs, 3, at room temperature

Whole milk, ½ cup (4 fl oz/125 ml)

Vanilla extract, 1 teaspoon

FOR THE WHIPPED CREAM

Cold heavy cream, 1 cup (8 fl oz/250 ml)

Confectioners' sugar, 2 tablespoons

MOLTEN CHOCOLATE CUPCAKES

MAKES 12 CUPCAKES

Call them cupcakes, mini cakes, or explosions of chocolate, but whatever you do, be sure to eat these cupcakes as soon as you can for maximum enjoyment (after about five minutes of cooling). Cut into a cake and watch as molten chocolate spills out from the inside. Serve them with a little whipped cream, tall glasses of milk, or as is.

1 Position a rack in the middle of the oven and preheat to 375°F (190°C). Lightly spray 12 standard muffin cups with cooking spray.

2 Place the chocolate and butter in a heatproof bowl. Microwave on low for 1 minute. Stir and continue to microwave on low in 30-second bursts, stirring in between intervals until the butter and chocolate are melted and smooth. Set aside to cool slightly. Whisk the egg yolks into the chocolate mixture until well combined, about 30 seconds. Add the flour and whisk until combined.

3 In a bowl, using an electric mixer on medium-high speed, beat the egg whites and salt until foamy. Slowly add the sugar, beating continuously, until soft peaks form (slightly bent tips when a beater is lifted). Using a whisk, gently fold a third of the egg whites into the chocolate mixture to lighten it. Fold in the egg white mixture in 2 more additions until no white streaks remain.

4 Spoon the batter into each muffin cup, filling it about two-thirds full. Bake the cupcakes for 5 minutes and then remove the pan from the oven; working quickly, insert one piece of bittersweet chocolate into the center of each cupcake. Return the pan to the oven and bake until the cupcakes are well risen and brown around the edges, 3–5 minutes more.

5 Let the cupcakes cool slightly in the pan on a wire rack, about 5 minutes. Use a small offset spatula to transfer cupcakes to plates and serve right away.

Nonstick cooking spray

Semisweet chocolate, 3½ oz (105 g), chopped

Unsalted butter, 4 tablespoons (½ stick/ 2 oz/60 g), cut into 4 pieces

Large eggs, 3, separated, at room temperature

Unbleached all-purpose flour, 2 tablespoons

Salt, pinch

Sugar, ¼ cup (2 oz/60 g)

Bittersweet chocolate bar, 1 (about 4 oz/125 g), broken evenly into 12 pieces

YEAST BREADS
& PIZZA

ALL ABOUT
YEAST BREADS
& PIZZA

What do focaccia, dinner rolls, and pizza have in common? Besides the fact that they're irresistible, they all start with a packet of yeast. Yeast is the substance that makes bread and pizza crust rise. Because it's a living thing, yeast needs lots of love and attention. But once you know what it likes, namely sugar and warmth, it's easy to work with.

Yeast doughs have two main things in common: They rely on yeast to help the dough rise; and they require kneading to combine the ingredients and create structure in the finished bread or crust.

The type of yeast we're using in this chapter needs to be activated, or "proofed," before incorporating it into a dough. Proofing begins by dissolving yeast in warm water. Sugar is often added to help excite the yeast. After about 10 minutes, the yeast mixture should be actively bubbling and foamy, and you know it's ready to use.

Flash forward to after the yeast has been incorporated into the dough. Now, instead of a gentle approach, you can be rough with it. The dough needs to be kneaded to develop the gluten in the flour and provide structure in the finished bread. The kneading phase requires some elbow grease and patience, but the process is rewarding as you feel the dough literally transforming in your hands. Consider this your workout before your imminent carb-eating!

BREAD BAKING FAQS

Q: Why can't I get my yeast to proof?
A: Your water may be too hot or too cold, or the yeast packet could be expired. Start over with new yeast.

Q: Why is my dough rising so fast?
A: Your kitchen could be too warm; move it to a cooler location.

Q: Why is my dough not rising?
A: Your kitchen could be too cool; transfer it to a warmer location.

WHAT YOU NEED

ASSORTED MIXING BOWLS

WOODEN SPOON

ELBOW GREASE

ROLLING PIN (OPTIONAL)

BAKING SHEET OR BAKING PAN

PASTRY BRUSH (OPTIONAL)

SECRETS TO SUCCESS

FIRE IT UP In order to get a crisp golden-brown crust, it's important to preheat the oven fully before baking bread or pizza. Turn the oven on 30–45 minutes before you plan to begin baking.

FEEL THE NEED TO KNEAD Kneading may seem like an awkward thing to do at first, but once you get into the press-fold-and-turn rhythm, it will start to feel natural and enjoyable.

TAKE THE TEMP Yeast needs warm water in order to thrive. Too hot and it will kill the yeast; too cold and it won't activate quickly. To reach an ideal temperature of 105°–115°F (40°–46°C), let your tap run warm for a minute or so and test the temperature with an instant-read thermometer.

PICK A WARM SPOT Yeast dough needs a warm, draft-free spot for rising. Think sunny pantries, on top of the dryer, near a hot oven, etc. The rising process can take 1–2 hours depending on the temperature of the room.

PATIENCE, PATIENCE Rolling or stretching pizza dough into shape takes time. If you feel like the dough is being stubborn and will no longer budge, let it rest for about 5 minutes to relax it, then give it another go.

SOME LIKE IT HOT

Yeast doughs bake best in really hot ovens. Yeast dough's initial contact with the heat produces an important reaction known as "oven spring," and that jolt of heat is essential for a high-rising, well-textured loaf or crust. It's important that your oven reaches the full temperature indicated in the recipe before baking the bread to be sure this oven spring is achieved.

HOW TO HANDLE
YEAST DOUGH

1
PROOF THE YEAST
Sprinkle the yeast over warm water in a bowl. (Some recipes call for adding sugar and/or oil, too.) Let it stand for 5–10 minutes, until foamy.

2
MAKE THE DOUGH
Mix the dough ingredients with a wooden spoon until a rough dough forms, adding more flour if needed if the dough feels excessively sticky.

3
KNEAD THE DOUGH
Put the dough on a floured work surface and knead until smooth and shiny, about 10 minutes, adding more flour if needed. The dough should be soft, but not sticky. Transfer to a lightly oiled bowl.

4

LET IT RISE

Cover the bowl loosely with plastic wrap and set it in a warm place until it doubles in bulk, 1–2 hours. When you're ready to use it, punch down the dough with your fist to deflate it.

5

SHAPE & BAKE

Shape the dough into the desired form. Some recipes will call for letting the dough rise a second time. Other recipes will call for baking right after shaping.

HOW TO MAKE
PIZZA DOUGH

Warm water (105°–115°F/ 40°–46°C), 1 cup (8 fl oz/250 ml)

Sugar, 1 teaspoon

Olive oil, 1 teaspoon

Active dry yeast, 1 package (2½ teaspoons)

Unbleached all-purpose flour, 1½ cups (7½ oz/235 g), plus more as needed

Salt, 1 teaspoon

In a bowl, stir together the warm water, sugar, and oil. Sprinkle the yeast on top and let stand until foamy, about 10 minutes. In a large bowl, using a wooden spoon, stir together the flour and the salt. Stir in the yeast mixture, gradually adding more flour if needed, to form a soft dough. Follow the directions at left to knead the dough and let it rise.

ONION, OLIVE & FETA PIZZA

MAKES 1 LARGE PIZZA

With this easy-to-make pizza recipe in your repertoire, you'll never go back to frozen pizza! Plus, once you've mastered the basic dough, you can create endless topping variations to suit your mood (or use up whatever's in the fridge). Because the toppings for this pizza are so full-flavored, a sauce is not necessary.

1 Follow the instructions on page 123 to make the pizza dough and let it rise.

2 Warm a large frying pan over medium heat and add the oil. Add the onions and reduce the heat to low. Add the water, tossing to coat. Cover and cook, stirring occasionally and adding more water if needed to prevent scorching, until the onions are tender, about 8 minutes. Uncover and raise the heat to medium-high. Cook, stirring, until all the moisture has evaporated and the onions begin to turn golden, about 5 minutes. Stir in the vinegar and oregano and season with salt and pepper. Cook for 1 minute, then turn off the heat and let cool completely.

3 Position a rack in the lower third of the oven and preheat to 450°F (230°C). Lightly oil a large rimmed baking sheet and dust it lightly with cornmeal.

4 On a lightly floured work surface, gently stretch or roll out the dough to fit the prepared pan; be patient, as it could take a few minutes to get it there. Transfer the dough to the pan. Spread the cheese evenly over the dough and top with the caramelized onions.

5 Bake the pizza until the crust is golden-brown, about 20 minutes. Sprinkle the pizza with the olives during the last 5–10 minutes of baking. Let the pizza cool slightly, then cut it into squares and serve right away.

Pizza Dough (page 123)

Olive oil, 1 tablespoon, plus oil for greasing

Red onions, 1 lb (500 g), thinly sliced

Water, 2 tablespoons

Red wine vinegar, 1 tablespoon

Dried oregano, 1 teaspoon

Salt and freshly ground pepper

Cornmeal, for dusting

Feta cheese, 2 cups (10 oz/315 g), crumbled

Pitted Kalamata olives, 12, halved

MEAT LOVERS' PIZZA

MAKES 1 LARGE PIZZA

This pizza satisfies a meat craving like nobody's business! Feel free to change up the suggested toppings. Use your favorite combo of meats, like hard salami, leftover shredded pork or beef, or cooked pancetta, aiming for 3–4 oz (90–125 g) total. A light dusting of Parmesan is all you need to let the meaty goodness shine through.

1 Follow the instructions on page 123 to make the pizza dough and let it rise.

2 Position a rack in the lower third of the oven and preheat to 450°F (230°C). Lightly oil a large rimmed baking sheet and dust lightly with cornmeal.

3 On a lightly floured work surface, gently stretch or roll out the dough to fit the prepared pan; be patient, as it could take a few minutes to get it there. Transfer the dough to the pan. Brush the edge of the dough with a light coating of oil. Spread the dough evenly with the marinara sauce, leaving a ½-inch (12-mm) border. Layer on the coppa, soppressata, and prosciutto, and then top with the Parmesan. Season to taste with pepper.

4 Bake the pizza until the crust is golden, 15–20 minutes. Let the pizza cool slightly, then cut it into squares and serve right away.

Pizza Dough (page 123)

Olive oil, for shaping and brushing

Cornmeal, for dusting

Marinara or tomato sauce (see page 128 or use purchased sauce), ¾ cup (6 fl oz/180 ml)

Coppa, 1 oz (30 g) thinly sliced, then torn into bite-sized pieces

Soppressata, 1 oz (30 g) thinly sliced, then torn into bite-sized pieces

Prosciutto, 1 oz (30 oz) thinly sliced, then torn into bite-sized pieces

Parmesan cheese, 2 oz (60 g), shaved with a vegetable peeler

Freshly ground pepper

{ **HOW TO: STRETCHING PIZZA DOUGH**
Few of us are talented enough to toss pizza dough in the air like a pizzaiolo. But using your hands is still the best way to work with the dough. Using your palms and fingers, push, pat, and press the dough outward from the center to make the desired shape, leaving the edge slightly thicker. If the dough seems stubborn, becoming too elastic and shrinking back as you work with it, cover it with a kitchen towel and allow it to rest for about 10 minutes before proceeding. Resting gives the gluten, the protein in the flour that is developed during kneading, a chance to relax so the dough becomes more workable.

PEPPERONI & MUSHROOM PIZZA

MAKES 1 LARGE PIZZA

This classic topping combo combines meaty cremini mushrooms with thin slices of salty pepperoni for a burst of umami. For a totally homemade pie, make your own marinara sauce (see note below)—it's easy! For the best flavor, pass up pre-shredded cheese; buy a large mozzarella ball and shred it yourself.

1 Follow the instructions on page 123 to make the pizza dough and let it rise.

2 Position a rack in the lower third of the oven and preheat to 450°F (230°C). Lightly oil a large rimmed baking sheet and sprinkle lightly with cornmeal.

3 Warm a frying pan over medium-high heat and add the 1 tablespoon oil. Add the mushrooms and sauté until they release their juices and are browned, about 8 minutes. Transfer to a bowl.

4 On a lightly floured work surface, gently stretch or roll out the dough to fit the prepared pan; be patient, as it could take a few minutes to get it there. Transfer the dough to the pan. Brush the edge of the dough with a light coating of oil. Spread the dough evenly with the marinara sauce, leaving a ½-inch (12-mm) border. Sprinkle the oregano and mozzarella over the sauce, and then top with the pepperoni, mushrooms, and Parmesan. Season to taste with pepper.

5 Bake the pizza until the crust is golden, 15–20 minutes. Let the pizza cool slightly, then cut it into squares and serve right away.

Pizza Dough (page 123)

Olive oil, 1 tablespoon, plus oil as needed

Cornmeal, for dusting

Cremini mushrooms, ½ lb (250 g), sliced

Freshly ground pepper

Marinara or tomato sauce (see below or use purchased sauce), ¾ cup (6 fl oz/ 180 ml)

Dried oregano, ¼ teaspoon

Low-moisture whole-milk mozzarella cheese, 2 oz (60 g), shredded

Thinly sliced pepperoni, 2 oz (60 g)

Parmesan cheese, 2 oz (60 g), shaved with a vegetable peeler

{ **HOW TO: QUICK MARINARA SAUCE**
In a frying pan over medium-high heat, warm 1 tablespoon olive oil. Add 1 clove minced garlic and sauté until golden, about 2 minutes. Add 1 can (15 oz/470 g) crushed tomatoes, bring to a boil, then reduce the heat to medium. Season with salt, pepper, and 1 tablespoon finely chopped fresh basil (optional) and simmer for 5–10 minutes.

ONION FOCACCIA

This Italian-style flatbread is perfect as a snack, served alongside soups and salads, or split and used for sandwiches. It's a dense, chewy bread, so it can be loaded up with toppings for endless variations. Strips of roasted red peppers, chopped fresh herbs, pitted olives, or red pepper flakes are great additions.

1 Pour the warm water into a small bowl and sprinkle with the yeast and sugar. Stir briefly, then let stand until foamy, about 10 minutes. In a large bowl, stir together the flour and salt. Add the yeast mixture along with ¼ cup (2 fl oz/60 ml) of the oil and stir with a wooden spoon until the dough forms a rough mass. Add the onion and stir until incorporated. Cover and let stand for 20 minutes.

2 Lightly oil a 9-by-13-inch (23-by-33-cm) pan. Transfer the dough to a lightly floured work surface. Using the heel of one hand, push the dough away from you and then pull it back with your fingertips. Turn and repeat to knead the dough until smooth and elastic, 5–7 minutes. Transfer the dough to the prepared pan, cover with plastic wrap and let the dough rise in a warm place until doubled in bulk, 1–1½ hours.

3 Position a rack in the lower third of the oven and preheat the oven to 450°F (230°C).

4 With your fingertips, make deep indentations 1 inch (2.5 cm) apart across the surface of the dough, almost to the bottom of the pan. Sprinkle evenly with the coarse salt and drizzle with the remaining ¼ cup (2 fl oz/60 ml) olive oil. Cover loosely with plastic and let rise at room temperature until puffy, about 30 minutes. Bake until golden-brown, 20–30 minutes. Cut into slices or squares and serve warm.

Warm water (105°–115°F/ 40°–46°C), 1¾ cups (14 fl oz/ 430 ml)

Active dry yeast, 2 packages (5 teaspoons)

Sugar, 1 teaspoon

Unbleached all-purpose flour, 5 cups (25 oz/780 g), plus flour as needed

Salt, 2 teaspoons

Olive oil, ½ cup (4 fl oz/ 120 ml), plus oil as needed

Yellow onion, ½ cup (2 oz/60 g), chopped

Coarse salt, 1 tablespoon

HERBED FOCACCIA

MAKES 1 LARGE FOCACCIA

This simple and delicious flatbread is amazing straight out of the oven,
but it will also keep fresh wrapped tightly in a brown paper bag
for up to five days. Any kind of fresh herb will do, but we suggest
a combination of thyme, rosemary, and oregano.

1 Pour the warm water into a small bowl and sprinkle with the yeast and sugar. Stir briefly, then let stand until foamy, about 10 minutes. In a large bowl, stir together the 5 cups (25 oz/780 g) flour and the salt. Add the yeast mixture along with ½ cup (4 fl oz/120 ml) of the oil and stir with a wooden spoon until the dough forms a rough mass. Cover and let stand for 10 minutes.

2 Lightly oil a 9-by-13-inch (23-by-33-cm) pan. Transfer the dough to a lightly floured work surface. Using the heel of one hand, push the dough away from you and then pull it back with your fingertips. Turn and repeat to knead the dough until smooth and elastic, 5–7 minutes. Transfer the dough to the prepared pan, cover with plastic wrap, and let the dough rise in a warm place until doubled in bulk, 1–1½ hours.

3 Position a rack in the lower third of the oven and preheat the oven to 450°F (230°C).

4 With your fingertips, make deep indentations 1 inch (2.5 cm) apart across the surface of the dough, almost to the bottom of the pan. Sprinkle evenly with the coarse salt and herbs and drizzle with the remaining ¼ cup (2 fl oz/60 ml) olive oil. Bake until golden, 20–30 minutes. Cut into slices or squares and serve warm.

Warm water (105°–115°F/ 40°–46°C), 1¾ cups (14 fl oz/ 430 ml)

Active dry yeast, 2 packages (5 teaspoons)

Sugar, 1 teaspoon

Unbleached all-purpose flour, 5 cups (25 oz/780 g), plus flour as needed

Salt, 2 teaspoons

Olive oil, ¾ cup (6 fl oz/180 ml)

Coarse salt, 1 tablespoon

Mixed fresh herbs, 1 teaspoon chopped

SPINACH CALZONES

MAKES 6 CALZONES

As turnovers are to fruit pies, calzones are to pizzas: inside-out pockets of goodness with hot, oozy filling inside a golden-brown crust. This version is filled with a mixture of creamy ricotta cheese and sautéed spinach and onions. Serve with a side of marinara sauce (see page 128) for dipping, if you like.

1 Follow the instructions on page 123 to make the pizza dough and let it rise.

2 Rinse the spinach thoroughly. In a large frying pan over medium heat, warm the 2 tablespoons oil. Add the onion and sauté until translucent, about 5 minutes. Stir in the garlic and cook until fragrant, about 1 minute. Add the spinach, cover, and cook until tender, about 3 minutes. Drain the spinach mixture in a colander and let cool. Press firmly on the spinach to remove as much excess liquid as you can. Transfer the mixture to a bowl. Add the Parmesan, mozzarella, and ricotta cheeses, and mix well. Season with salt and pepper.

3 Position racks in the center and lower third of the oven and preheat to 400°F (200°C). Oil 2 large rimmed baking sheets. Divide the pizza dough into 6 equal portions, and shape each portion into a ball. Place the balls on a work surface and cover with a kitchen towel.

4 Place 1 dough ball on a lightly floured work surface. Using a rolling pin, roll out the dough into a round 7 inches (18 cm) in diameter. Brush the dough edges lightly with water. Place one-sixth of the spinach-cheese mixture on half of the round, leaving a 1-inch (2.5-cm) border. Fold the dough over so the edges meet, then crimp the edges with a fork. Pierce the top of the calzone with the fork and transfer to a prepared baking sheet. Repeat with the remaining dough and filling, putting 3 calzones on each baking sheet. Brush the calzones with olive oil. Bake until golden, about 20 minutes.

5 Transfer the calzones to a wire rack and let cool for 10 minutes (the filling will be too hot to eat right away). Serve warm.

Double batch of Pizza Dough (page 123)

Baby spinach, 10 oz (315 g)

Olive oil, 2 tablespoons, plus oil as needed

Yellow onion, 1, finely chopped

Garlic, 2 cloves, finely chopped

Parmesan cheese, ½ cup (2 oz/60 g) grated

Fresh mozzarella cheese, ¼ lb (125 g), finely diced

Ricotta cheese, 1 cup (½ lb/250 g)

Kosher salt and freshly ground pepper

Flour, for dusting

BACON, CARAMELIZED ONION & GRUYÈRE FLATBREAD

MAKES 1 LARGE FLATBREAD

Rich with olive oil, Gruyère cheese, smoky thick-cut bacon, and sweet onions, this bread is like taking a quick trip to France, where the flavor trio rules all over the northern region of the country. Eat it like a pizza for a snack, or add a green salad and call it a meal.

1 Pour the warm water into a small bowl and sprinkle with the yeast and 1 teaspoon of the sugar. Stir briefly, then let stand until foamy, about 10 minutes. In a large bowl, stir together the flour and salt. Add the yeast mixture along with the 6 tablespoons (3 fl oz/90 ml) oil and stir with a wooden spoon until the dough forms a rough mass. Cover and let stand for 10 minutes.

2 Transfer the dough to a lightly floured work surface. Using the heel of one hand, push the dough away from you and then pull it back with your fingertips. Turn and repeat to knead the dough until smooth and elastic, 5–7 minutes. Form the dough into a ball, place in a lightly oiled bowl, and turn to coat. Cover the bowl with plastic wrap and let the dough rise in a warm spot until doubled in bulk, about 1 hour.

3 In a frying pan over medium heat, sauté the bacon until crisp. Transfer the bacon to paper towels. Pour off most of the fat in the pan, then add the onions and sauté until softened, about 3 minutes. Stir in the remaining 1 teaspoon sugar and a pinch of salt and cook until the onions are deep-golden, about 20 minutes. Stir in the bacon, and cool.

4 Lightly oil a large rimmed baking sheet. Pour the dough onto the prepared pan. Using your fingers, stretch the dough into a rectangle about 10-by-14 inches (25-by-35 cm). Cover the dough loosely with a kitchen towel and let rise in a warm place until puffy, about 1 hour.

5 Preheat the oven to 425°F (220°C). Dimple the surface of the dough with your fingertips. Gently brush the dough with oil, then sprinkle evenly with the bacon-onion mixture and cheese. Bake until golden, 15–18 minutes. Cut into squares and serve warm.

Warm water (105°–115°F/ 40°–46°C), 1 cup (8 fl oz/ 250 ml)

Active dry yeast, 1 package (2½ teaspoons)

Sugar, 2 teaspoons

Unbleached all-purpose flour, 3 cups (15 oz/470 g)

Salt, 1 teaspoon, plus salt as needed

Olive oil, 6 tablespoons (3 fl oz/90 ml), plus oil as needed

Applewood-smoked bacon, 6 thick slices, cut crosswise into ½-inch (12-mm) slices

Yellow onions, 2, halved and thinly sliced

Gruyère cheese, 1 cup (4 oz/125 g) shredded

PITA BREAD

Just say no to doughy, dried-out, breaks-when-you-fill-it, purchased pita. Invite your friends over for a pita party and watch as they marvel when the dough rounds puff dramatically in the high heat of the oven. Stuff the pitas with your favorite sandwich ingredients or cut into triangles for dipping into hummus and other dips.

1 Pour the warm water into a small bowl and sprinkle with the yeast and sugar. Stir briefly, then let stand until foamy, about 10 minutes. In a large bowl, stir together the flour and the salt. Add the yeast mixture along with the 2 tablespoons oil and stir with a wooden spoon until the dough forms a rough mass. Cover and let stand for 10 minutes.

2 Transfer the dough to a lightly floured work surface. Using the heel of one hand, push the dough away from you and then pull it back with your fingertips. Turn and repeat to knead the dough until smooth and elastic, 5–7 minutes. Form the dough into a ball, place in a lightly oiled bowl, and turn to coat. Cover the bowl with plastic wrap and let rise in a warm place until doubled in bulk, 1–1½ hours.

3 Preheat the oven to 450°F (230°C). Turn the dough out onto a lightly floured work surface and divide it in half. Cover half with plastic wrap. Divide the remaining half into 5 equal pieces and form each piece into a ball. Let rest for 10 minutes while dividing the other dough portion. Using a lightly floured rolling pin, roll out the balls into rounds about 6 inches (15 cm) in diameter and ¼-inch (6-mm) thick. If the dough does not roll out easily, let it rest, covered, for 10 minutes. Drape each round over the rolling pin and transfer it to a floured kitchen towel. Cover with another towel and let rest until puffy, about 15 minutes.

4 Preheat a baking sheet in the oven for 6 minutes. Quickly brush the sheet with oil. Transfer 3 or 4 dough rounds to the hot sheet and place it in the oven. Do not open the oven door for 3 minutes. Bake until puffed and light brown, 6–7 minutes. Stack the pitas on a plate and cover with a kitchen towel. Bake the remaining pitas, then serve warm or at room temperature.

Warm water (105°–115°F/ 40°–46°C), 1½ cups (12 fl oz/375 ml)

Active dry yeast, 1 package (2½ teaspoons)

Sugar, 1 teaspoon

Unbleached all-purpose flour, 3½–4 cups (17½–20 oz/545–625 g), plus flour as needed

Salt, 1½ teaspoons

Olive oil, 2 tablespoons, plus oil as needed

HERBED BREADSTICKS

Serving crisp sticks of homemade bread makes any meal a little more special. Start your meal dipping them into good-quality olive oil seasoned with salt and pepper. For a cheesy twist, sprinkle the sticks with grated Parmesan before baking. Look for Italian semolina flour, also used to make pasta, in a speciality food store.

1 Pour the warm water into a small bowl and sprinkle with the yeast and the sugar. Stir briefly, then let stand until foamy, about 10 minutes. In a large bowl, stir together the all-purpose and semolina flours, salt, and thyme. Add the yeast mixture along with the 3 tablespoons oil and stir with a wooden spoon until the dough forms a rough mass. Cover and let stand for 10 minutes.

2 Transfer the dough to a lightly floured work surface. Using the heel of one hand, push the dough away from you and then pull it back with your fingertips. Turn and repeat to knead the dough until smooth and elastic, 5–7 minutes.

3 Sprinkle a cutting board with semolina flour. Pat the dough on the board into a 14-by-8-inch (35-by-20-cm) rectangle. Brush the dough with oil. Cover loosely with plastic wrap and let rise on the board in a warm place until doubled in bulk, 1–1½ hours.

4 Preheat the oven to 375°F (190°C). Line three large rimmed baking sheets with parchment paper and brush the paper with oil.

5 Rub the surface of the dough with a few tablespoons of semolina flour. With a sharp knife, cut the dough crosswise into 4 equal portions. One at a time, cut each portion lengthwise into 8 strips. Pick up the end of each strip and stretch and roll to the width of a prepared sheet. Place the strips ½ inch (12 mm) apart on the sheets.

6 One at a time, place the sheets in the oven and bake until the bread sticks are lightly browned and crisp, 16–22 minutes. Transfer to racks to cool completely. Serve at room temperature.

Warm water (105°–115°F/ 40°–46°C), 1½ cups (12 fl oz/375 ml)

Active dry yeast, 1 package (2½ teaspoons)

Sugar, ½ teaspoon

Unbleached all-purpose flour, 3–3½ cups (15–17½ oz/470–545 g), plus flour as needed

Semolina flour, ½ cup (2½ oz/75 g), plus flour as needed

Salt, 1½ teaspoons

Dried thyme, 1½ teaspoons

Olive oil, 3 tablespoons, plus oil as needed

DINNER ROLLS

MAKES 16 ROLLS

Patience is key when making these moist, rich buns. The dough needs to rise
twice: once as a large ball, and again after shaping into individual rolls,
but it's worth it for the tender, buttery result. Serve the rolls as a side dish
for any meal, or split them to make mini sandwiches for a game day party.

1 Pour the warm water into a small bowl and sprinkle with the yeast and sugar. Stir briefly, then let stand until foamy, about 10 minutes. In a large bowl, stir together the flour and salt. Add the yeast mixture along with the milk, 2 eggs, and butter and mix with a wooden spoon until the dough forms a rough mass. Cover and let stand for 10 minutes.

2 Transfer the dough to a lightly floured work surface. Using the heel of one hand, push the dough away from you and then pull it back with your fingertips. Turn and repeat to knead the dough until smooth and elastic, 5–7 minutes. Form the dough into a ball, place in a lightly oiled bowl, and turn to coat. Cover with plastic wrap and let the dough rise in a warm place until doubled in bulk, 1½–2 hours.

3 Generously butter two 9-inch (23-cm) round cake pans. Punch down the dough and turn it out onto a clean work surface. Cut the dough in half with a sharp knife. Cut each dough half into 8 equal pieces. Roll each piece against the work surface into a round ball. Put the balls in the prepared pans, placing 7 balls around the edge and 1 ball in the center of each. Cover loosely with a kitchen towel and let rise until puffy and pillow-soft when gently squeezed, 30–40 minutes.

4 Position a rack in the lower third of the oven and preheat to 400°F (200°C). Brush the dough balls lightly with the beaten egg. (You may not use all of the egg.) Bake until the rolls are puffed and golden, 20–25 minutes. Serve warm.

Warm water (105°–115°F/ 40°–46°C), ¼ cup (2 fl oz/ 60 ml)

Active dry yeast, 1 package (2½ teaspoons)

Sugar, 2 tablespoons

Unbleached all-purpose flour, 4½ cups (22½ oz/ 705 g), plus flour as needed

Salt, 2 teaspoons

Whole milk, 1 cup (8 fl oz/250 ml)

Eggs, 2, at room temperature, plus 1 egg, lightly beaten, for brushing

Unsalted butter, 6 tablespoons (3 oz/90 g), cut into cubes, at room temperature

INDEX

weldonowen

415 Jackson Street, Suite 200, San Francisco, CA 94111
www.weldonowen.com

BAKE GOOD THINGS
Conceived and produced by Weldon Owen, Inc.
In collaboration with Williams-Sonoma, Inc.
3250 Van Ness Avenue, San Francisco, CA 94109

A WELDON OWEN PRODUCTION
Printed and bound in China by 1010 Printing, Ltd.

First printed in 2014
10 9 8 7 6 5 4 3 2 1

Library of Congress Control Number:
2013956569

ISBN 13: 978-1-61628-767-2
ISBN 10: 1-61628-767-5

WELDON OWEN, INC.
CEO and President Terry Newell
VP, Sales and Marketing Amy Kaneko
VP, Publisher Roger Shaw

Associate Publisher Jennifer Newens
Assistant Editor Emma Rudolph

Creative Director Kelly Booth
Art Director Alisha Petro
Designer Rachel Lopez Metzger

Production Director Chris Hemesath
Production Manager Michelle Duggan

Photographer Eva Kolenko
Food Stylist Erin Quon
Prop Stylist Esther Feinman

Weldon Owen is a division of
BONNIER

ACKNOWLEDGMENTS

Weldon Owen wishes to thank the following people for their generous support in producing this book:
Jane Tunks Demel, Brian Lackey, Ashley Lima, Lori Nunokawa, Elizabeth Parson, and Alexa Weibel